CHRISTEL MOUCHARD

FOREWORD AND INTRODUCTIONS
BY ALEXANDRA LAPIERRE

Women Travelers

A Century of Trailblazing Adventures
1850–1950

Flammarion

Contents

Why They Set Out 4

Out of the Ordinary *Before 1850* 6

Catalina de Erauso *Spanish* 10

Aphra Behn *English* 14

Isabel Godin des Odonais *French-Peruvian* 18

Trekking in Crinolines *1850–90* 22

How They Survived 24

The Blessings of a Good Thick Skirt 28

Ida Pfeiffer *Austrian* 30

Alexine Tinne *Dutch* 36

Mary Seacole *Jamaican* 44

Florence Baker *Hungarian* 52

Isabella Bird *Scottish* 58

May French-Sheldon *American* 64

Marianne North *English* 70

Jane Dieulafoy *French* 74

Fanny Stevenson *American* 82

Mary Kingsley *English* 88

Fanny Bullock Workman *American* 94

Between Two Worlds *1890–18* 100

Why They Wrote 102

With the Tip of a Parasol 106

Gertrude Bell *English* 108

Margaret Fountaine *English* 116

Daisy Bates *Irish* 122

Nellie Bly *American* 130

Isabelle Eberhardt *Swiss-Russian-French* 136

Charmian Kittredge *American* 142

Alexandra David-Néel *French* 150

Free and Easy *1918–50* 158

The Way They Loved 160

A Scent of Liberty 164

Freya Stark *English* 166

Karen Blixen *Danish* 172

Evelyn Cheesman *English* 180

Rosita Forbes *English* 186

Margaret Mead *American* 192

Ella Maillart *Swiss* 200

Osa Johnson *American* 208

Odette du Puigaudeau *French* 214

Anita Conti *French* 220

Emily Hahn *American* 228

Indefatigable! 234

Notes 236

Selected Bibliography 237

Photographic Credits 238

Why They Set Out

"Obedience means death!"

By choosing these words to begin her very first book, titled *Pour la vie* (For Life), Alexandra David-Néel had already said it all. With this maxim she challenged popular beliefs, she linked adventure to a written formula, she shed light on her own path, and she recounted—in one line—the whole history of this book.

These women's curiosity about the world and their quest to find their own truth required one particular type of courage: the courage to disobey. How can "adventure" be declined in the feminine? Whereas the term adventurer suggests a passion for new frontiers, the term adventuress suggests neither departure, nor travel, nor great distance; rather, it connotes ambitiousness, intrigue, mercenary sex. Even in the twentieth century, when "adventure" assumed the connotation that André Malraux explicitly gave it in French—"venturing further"—women who "set off for the unknown" could not be called adventuresses; another term had to be coined if great women explorers were to be distinguished from the horde of courtesans and spies. Yet even a new coinage would have been a waste of breath, for Malraux himself quipped: "Men have adventures, women have lovers!"

To men, then, was allocated the conquest of the world; to women, the conquest of men.

Yet how could it have been otherwise? From the dawn of time right up to the 1950s—in the Latin countries of southern Europe, at least—women *belonged*, in the strict sense of the term, to the men of the family. They belonged legally to their fathers while still maidens, to their husbands once they were married, and finally to their sons once they were widowed.

Considered minors all their lives, women could not sign contracts, acquire or sell property, travel, or even make a living without the consent of a man. Breaking this law meant running every risk, including the risk of losing everything: her place in the world, her husband, her children, her family, her social and professional status, her happiness. "What happiness?" exploded Freya Stark, the explorer who discovered, on her own, the Valley of the Assassins in central Iran

in 1930. "There can be no happiness if the things we believe in are different from the things we do." So what did Stark hope to find in life? What, for her, was real life, the only one worth living?

"You don't even need to hope in order to venture," pointed out the travel writer Annemarie Schwarzenbach in a somewhat more sorrowful mode, "nor succeed in order to persevere." Meanwhile, Odette du Puigaudeau, who crossed the Mauritanian desert in bare feet, claimed that she "liked this uncivilized life, where [she was] neither man nor woman, but just a human being who stands on its own two legs."

What did these three twentieth-century pioneers share with all other female trailblazers? A sense of curiosity, obviously. A feeling of not belonging to the society that surrounded them, certainly. A quenchless thirst for truth. But also fear—the bottomless fear of never being able to fulfill themselves. They shared the same need to stand out, the same boundless pride, the same loneliness. But what is the connection between Karen Blixen, who wrote *Out of Africa,* and Catalina Erauso, Spain's seventeenth-century warrior-nun? Or between Alexine Tinne, a flamboyant Dutch aristocrat who camped in the Egyptian desert among her servants and camels, and Margaret Fountaine, a butterfly-hunting spinster in the Amazon? What do they all share—across space and time—all these women with their very different personalities? One special talent, at the very least: to recognize their own instincts, to nurture their own desires. And not let anyone—nor any thing, any idea, any fear—lead them astray or starve their souls. They knew how to "go for it."

Karen Blixen, Freya Stark, Odette du Puigaudeau, Catalina de Erauso, Alexine Tinne, Margaret Fountaine, and all the women described in this book decided to stand on their own two feet. Such was their strength, their special quality.

But in order to acquire this unusual autonomy, in order to become footloose—an independence of heart and mind that would carry them to the ends of the earth—all these women, even the

most conventional, most well-behaved, and most pious, had to start by saying "No!"

The learning curve was steep.

The first generation of rebels was one of *survivors,* whose only option was to flee.

Flee is what Catalina de Erauso did when faced with Spanish religious authorities in the days of the Inquisition: she escaped from the convent where her father had placed her, fled across all of Spain, sailed the oceans, fought the Indians in the New World, and hid herself behind so many male identities that even her female lovers and admirers wound up losing track of her.

Flee is what England's Aphra Behn did when she traveled through Holland and explored Surinam in search of fame and fortune, signing letters with phony names, until the day she found herself in prison in London, only to enjoy her final resting place in a vault in Westminster Abbey, the sole woman in history to be accorded this honor.

And flee is what Isabel Godin des Odonais did when she crossed the Amazonian forest in order to save her own life.

The second generation, the one of crinoline-clad trekkers, would be more cautious—or at least, more patient—when it came to flouting the conventions that constrained them. Before setting sail, Queen Victoria's contemporaries waited docilely until life's vagaries freed them from their duty to loved ones. It was mourning that opened new paths to them—the death of a father, the loss of a husband or brother. As a result, such women set out later in life. Mary Kingsley, for example, spent the first thirty years of her life caring for her unwell mother. Isabella Bird and Marianne North were forty before they began traveling. But once on the road, there was no stopping them. These spinsters and respectable widows would no more turn back than did the fugitive generation that had won its freedom by the blade of a sword. And woe betide anyone who tried to hold them back, for they had learned that life was only worth what they were able to grasp of it. They knew how to defend themselves. "Although I was fully aware that all the chambers of my pistol were loaded, I studied the barrel, very pointedly," recounted Miss Bird. "The effect was just as desired." And they also know how to attack, "Every man who is not on his feet . . . when I have counted three, I will shoot!" exclaimed May French-Sheldon.

The idiotic cruelty of two world wars allowed the next two generations to move forward, although in fits and starts: one step into the future, another back into the past, yet another into crisis. Above all, new questions loomed. How could emotional ties be squared with the call of the wild? Or marital ties with freedom? Or motherhood with absence? As the oceanographer Anita Conti put it, "Make love, sure, but don't make babies!"

But how can you deal with conjugal life without rejecting it completely?

Like their predecessors, who waited until a loved one died before setting out, some of these women would wait until their children had grown. And yet their obsession with the quest for truth, a quest affecting life, death, and roots, marginalized them and set them apart.

How could they face solitude, how could they bear it and inflict it on loved ones without being swallowed up by it? There was one good way: become a link in the long chain of acquired human knowledge. Report what they had seen. Bear witness to the incredible dream that spurs humanity to defy illness and death, to discover unknown continents, to plant flags on inaccessible peaks.

What distinguished these trailblazers from hundreds of travelers and countless tourists is the way they passed on their experiences—by writing about them. "In the end, and before everything else," allegedly claimed Ella Maillart, who scaled tall peaks, "the best way to rid yourself of an obsessive desire is to fulfill it!"

Alexandra Lapierre

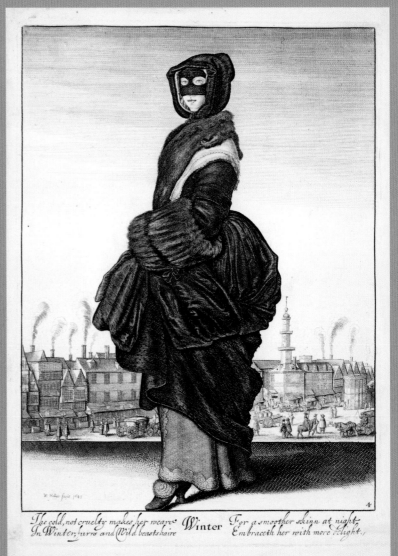

The cold, not cruelty makes her weare Winter For a smoother skinn at night,
In Winter, furrs and Wild beasts haire   Embraceth her with more delight.

4

Out of the Ordinary

It is customary to date the earliest female explorations to the 1850s. It was not that women didn't have a desire to travel before that time—they've always had it, as we know from the few names that have risen from the timeless depths of history to the surface of today, names that chroniclers present as oddities, as something to be put on show, as "freaks" even.

"The eternally fantastical figure
of the woman in a page's clothing"

Christel Mouchard

Freaks when they dressed like men. The eternally fantastical figure of the woman in a page's clothing has haunted literature, dreams, and tales of travels. Phony soldiers, phony sailors, phony cowboys—dozens of names could be mentioned, although most of the turncoats will remain anonymous forever. In his memoirs, the explorer Henry Morton Stanley recounted how, when he himself was a vagrant child who had just arrived in New Orleans, he shared a room with a lad who turned out to be a lassie. Kit Carson, the famous trapper, told a similar anecdote that occurred the first time he crossed the Great Plains. Many females crossed this boundary through necessity, in order to survive, to flee—or follow—a man. Some of them, however, did it through desire, through a rejection of their female body. Strangely, these women tended to win better acceptance.

Freaks when they refused to respect conventional morality. Spies and courtesans as well as travelers, such women crossed frontiers as often as men, hiding their tracks as often as they shuffled the decks at card tables where they squandered the money supplied by their powerful protectors. It was these women who gave the term "adventuress" its scandalous connotation, a meaning that the virtuous voyagers of the nineteenth century hoped to imbue with some honor.

Freaks, too, when they survived where men succumbed. Being able to cross, alone, an ice field or tropical forest—barefoot, without food or clothing—was an ability allegedly limited to the stronger sex. Once shipwrecked, children and women should normally die first—if the opposite happened, the order of things was turned upside down. The chronicler studied such creatures, wondered about such exceptions at length, simultaneously amazed and worried, forgetting that the order of things exists more in the mind than in deeds. The history of emigrations demonstrates as much—far from being rare, such "survivors" were myriad, modest, yet amazing adventurers, anonymous heroines lost in the vast population movements that swept the continents.

$\mathcal{I}$n the year 1607 a fifteen-year-old girl, dressed as a novice nun, huddled alone in the woods not far from the city of San Sebastian in northern Spain. Bent over a piece of stitching, she sewed intently—"like a well-behaved girl," people tend to say when it comes to girls and needlework. Yet Catalina de Erauso was not sewing like a well-behaved little girl. She had just fled the convent where her family had placed her, and now she was hastily concocting the male garments that were to be her gateway to freedom.

From her outer habit she fashioned breeches, from her petticoat she made a doublet and gaiters. In a final, radical act, she cut her hair.

Thus began a life of roaming, made possible by a not very feminine physique and by the casual recruitment of armies at the time. Hired as a page on several occasions, Erauso never stayed long in one place—she was too quarrelsome to conform to any discipline, as she herself acknowledged. Most of the time—strangely—she remained within the family orbit, in the home of an uncle or brother, which suggests that her real identity was not as secret as she would later claim in her memoirs. The people around her probably realized early on that she would never make a proper lady.

Sometime around 1615, Erauso crossed the Atlantic. Yet she remained within a familiar culture, because at that time Spain had the largest empire in the world, the one on which "the sun never set." Peru, a vast province covering the entire northwest of South America, was the heart of this Eldorado, from which a swarm of gold-laden galleons would set sail—only to be furiously attacked by rival nations. That was where Catalina first took part in combat, when the Spanish fleet was confronted by a Dutch squadron off Cartagena in Colombia. She found the odor of gunpowder so appealing that she decided to enlist in a regiment leaving for Chile, where she battled rebellious Indians for nearly ten years. When in the midst of battle she recovered the ensign snatched by the enemy, at the cost of three wounds to herself, she earned the nickname that would go down in Spanish history, the Ensign Nun (sometimes known in English as the Lieutenant Nun). Briefly put in charge of an entire company, she was relieved of all command when she hanged an Indian who happened

Pages 10 and 11: The siege of Cuzco, depicted by Francisco Pizarro; and an engraved portrait of Catalina de Erauso on her departure for New Spain, based on a painting by Francisco Pacheco.

Above: Battle scene, Peruvian school.

Facing page: Old view of Cuzco, Peru; and the Chilean Cordillera, by an anonymous artist.

to be—and here was her true crime—a Christian. Later, for obscure reasons, the Ensign Nun was forced to flee the army and continue wandering, this time down the Andes.

There is no point in repeating here all the details of Erauso's autobiography. It is so florid, so full of scuffles, duels, flights, mistaken identities, and banter, so similar to picaresque literature that the authenticity of everything it recounts can only be doubted. Nevertheless, the basic outlines must be accurate, since witnesses at the time described the incredible character of Erauso. One such witness was Fray Diego de Sevilla, who declared in a statement that he had met *la Monja al Farez* (the Ensign Nun), who was then calling herself Don Antonio de Erauso, and who owned negroes and mules with which she transported merchandise and baggage to various places (including Mexico City, to which his own affairs were shipped). She was considered to be a knight of great heart and skill. "She went around in men's clothing, wore a dagger and a sword with silver hilt, and knew how to use them."

The date of Erauso's death is unknown, but her memoirs, which she dictated in 1626 while in Rome seeking a papal audience in hopes of obtaining permission to live as a man, have come down through the centuries. Although not published until two hundred years later, her memoirs have since been translated into many languages, and adapted for stage and screen.[1] "She never had evil intentions," wrote a pilgrim monk, Pedro de La Valle, who met her in 1626, "but her calling was to the sword and freedom."

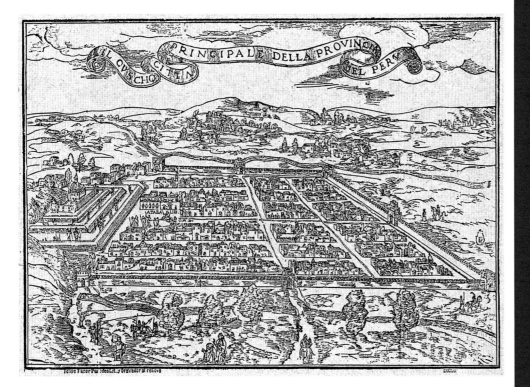

Never took a bath

The lady has no breasts,
and she told me she had used
I no longer recall what remedy
to dry them up, leaving her
as flat as a board. She also
said she never took a bath
and that she tried to adopt
men's manners.

Pedro de La Valle,
quoted in Marie Dronsart,
Les Grandes Voyageuses
(Paris: Hachette, 1894).

$\mathcal{T}$he seventeenth-century
adventuress needed to have
a shadowy past in which
she could deliberately cloak
herself. That was part of the
role—she was expected to lie
a little. What mattered, in the
end, was that people no longer
knew quite who she was, that
all that remained of her was an
impression of beauty and mystery.

Thus we now know that Behn was an authentic traveler and a real spy, before becoming one of the finest playwrights of her day.

Why did this free woman claim that she came from an aristocratic family, she who was born to a barber and a wet nurse in 1640? Why did she say that she left for Surinam because her father was appointed governor there, when in fact the family was far too modest to have ever made such a journey? Probably because the famous writer that she had become in her mature years might have had noble doors shut in her face if she admitted that she had gone alone to such a wild, distant colony. As to how a barber's daughter came to speak, write, and dress like a true lady, no biographer has yet been able to explain.

Attractive, educated, poor, and alone—the range of professions potentially practiced by the young traveler was narrow: spy or courtesan. As subsequent events would indicate, it is probable that Aphra Johnson (as she was known then) was sent on a mission to the colony in 1663 by the patent holder, Lord Willoughby, to observe the power struggle then taking place between the governor and the colonists. She certainly didn't go there with blinkers on her eyes: the novel that she based on her experience there, *Oroonoko,* described the condition of slaves, the tyranny of governors far from home, and the mixture of luxury, vulnerability, and wretched hygiene typical of those fragile, uncertain, unlikely little colonies.[2] But we should not

Pages 14 and 15: The slave trade in Surinam;
and a portrait of Aphra Behn aged approximately
thirty, by Mary Beale.

Above: The conditions to which slaves were
subjected in Surinam led them to rebel.

Facing page: Posthumous engraving dated 1716.

indulge in anachronism here—Aphra Behn was no forerunner of
the anti-slavery movement nor of exotic literature, contrary to what
was written about her two hundred years later. Her novel is in fact
an ultra-royalist allegory published at a time when the king of
England was threatened by partisans of the pretender, William of
Orange. Aphra moreover married a slave trader, the Dutchman
Johan Behn, who died the very next year, in 1665, leaving his
twenty-five-year-old widow free to pursue her career. It was also as
a faithful royalist that she was dispatched to Holland, again as a
secret agent, in 1667. This time, the archives have preserved a
record of her voyage; her mission, we read, was to evaluate the
information that a double agent was seeking to sell to the Crown.
The agent, an English adventurer by the name of Scot, claimed to
be in possession of secret files on the army in Holland, but London
strongly suspected him of being in the service of the powerful
enemy he was allegedly spying on. Behn—code named "Astrea"—
was instructed to ascertain whether the informer was a traitor.
According to the report she sent to her employer, although Scot
had initially been highly reserved on their first encounter, he soon
became "extremely willing" to answer her questions. This change
of heart was due not merely to the female agent's eloquence. Behn
overlooked no weapon, and would not disdain from using her
charms even though she denied the label of courtesan.

Behn probably hoped that her mission would earn her, if not a
fortune, at least the gratitude of her monarch and therefore a key

Riley Pinx.   R.W.fc.

Mrs Behn.

post at court. But she lost everything: not even having been reim-
bursed for her expenses, she was thrown into debtors' prison on her
return to London. It is probable that she failed to accomplish her
mission—there are hints that she was not indifferent to Scot's own
charms. Falling in love is a professional error that spies—and kept
women—can hardly afford.

Once freed, "Astrea" kept the wolf from the door by writing.
Her bold, lively style finally won her what she had so hoped to
obtain by political espionage. Her first play, *The Forc'd Marriage*, was
an instant hit, followed by other successful plays, all with a flavor of
libertinage. She died in 1689, admired and popular, the darling of
the rich and powerful, not long after the Glorious Revolution over-
threw the absolute monarchy she had so boldly defended, thereby
ushering in the British democracy she so detested.

*P*aint and powder
for ammunition

To a "worm-eaten" Dutch ship-
ping merchant, Van Bruin, who
courted the lady in hopes of
making her his mistress,
"Astrea" replied:
"Have you set before the Eyes
of your Understanding, the
charge of fitting out such a
Vessel (as you have made me)
for the Indies of Love. . . There
are Ribbonds and Hoods for my
Pennons; Diamond Rings,
Lockets, and Pearl-Necklaces
for my guns of Offence and
Defence; Silks, Holland, Lawn,
Cambrick, &c., for Rigging;
Gold and Silver Laces,
Imbroideries and Fringes fore
and aft for my Stern and for my
Prow; rich Perfumes, Paint and
Powder, for my Ammunition;
Treats, rich Wines, expensive
Collations, Gaming Money,
Pin-Money, with a long *Et cetera*
for my Cargo; and Balls, Masks,
Plays, Walks, Airing in the
Country, and a Coach and Six
for my fair Wind."

Quoted in Janet Todd, *The Secret Life of
Aphra Behn* (London: Pandora Press,
2000).

 sabel Godin was a loving wife. At least, that's what we can infer from the fact that, separated from her husband by over two thousand miles of unexplored Amazonian forest, she swore to get back to him whatever the cost. Isabel was in Peru, while her husband, Jean Godin des Odonais, was in French Guiana, on the Atlantic coast of South America.

Isabel Godin des Odonais

Surviving

The king of France and an interest in science had been jointly responsible for their marriage and their subsequent separation. Thirty-five years earlier, in 1734, a geographic mission commissioned by Louis XV sent Godin to Peru under the command of Charles de La Condamine. There, in 1742 the young Frenchman married the thirteen year-old Isabel de Casamayor y Bruno, who came from a grand Peruvian family.

Eight years later, Godin decided to return to France to settle questions of family inheritance. His wife was expected to join him as soon as he could arrange passage. But when he reached Cayenne in French Guiana, Jean found himself blocked by various political upheavals. He decided to settle in the region. Time went by—twenty-one years, to be exact. Then, in 1769, following the death of her only daughter, Isabel decided to rejoin her husband without waiting any longer. She and her brothers organized an expedition that would reach the Atlantic by navigating down the tributaries of the Amazon. In short order, the adventure turned into catastrophe: the missions in which the travelers expected to stay were found to be empty, due to the expulsion of the Jesuits, and the region was ravaged by smallpox. The rafts thus continued their route downriver, without food or supplies, until they ran aground on the Bobonaza River. The survivors set up camp, but no help arrived. They attempted to travel along the riverbank, but death overtook them one by one, until Isabel's seven companions had all died.

Thus she found herself alone, lost in the Amazonian jungle, with no supplies, her dress in tatters. She might have just let herself die. Many other people in her predicament would do just that. But not

Pages 18 and 19: Picturesque view of the Amazonian forest by the Comte de Clarac; and a portrait of Isabel Godin des Odonais by Chevignard (for *Le Magasin Pittoresque*, 1854).

Above, clockwise: View of Lima's Black suburb (engraved by Paolo Fumigalli); a forest scene; and Caripuna Indians with a tapir, 19th century (Franz Keller, *The Amazon and Madeira Rivers*, 1874).

Facing page: After an outbreak of smallpox, Isabel travels alone through the forest, trying to reach her husband.

Isabel Godin. She removed the shoes from her dead companions, made a pair of sturdy sandals, and headed alone into the forest. Some eight to ten days later, having eaten wild fruit and eggs snatched from nests, wracked by fever and open sores, she spotted a dugout canoe on the river, paddled by two Indians. They took care of her, taking her as far as the nearest mission. Within a matter of months, she had recovered and reached her husband, and later made it to France.

The various tellers of this tale concluded that such a trial could not befall a woman without mortally maiming her.[1] If they are to be believed, Isabel Godin des Odonais lived out her days as a mere ghost of herself, haunted by her horrible experiences. But the date of her death—1792—invites skepticism. "Isabel the Creole" lived for another twenty-three years, which is pretty good going. And it is hard to believe that luck alone was the only reason for her amazing ability to survive. Unfortunately, no one thought to question her on the details of her everyday life in the forest: how she hunted, spent the night, marched onward, struggled at every moment. Even the information supplied by her husband is succinct.[2] Therefore we can only imagine the cool-headed behavior—taking her dead brothers' boots, sleeping alone under the tall, rain-dripping trees, plunging her hands into birds' nests, scratching at the soil with her fingers. Although unplanned and unwanted, Isabel's adventure was a wonderful forerunner to the solitary exploits carried out by female trailblazers one hundred years later.

Her hair turned white

The recollection of the long, appalling spectacle she witnessed, the horror of the solitude and the nights in the wilderness, the fear of death always before her eyes, a fear that doubled with every passing minute, had such an effect upon her that her hair turned white.

Jean Godin des Odonais,
Letter to Charles de La Condamine,
Paris, 1778

21

1850–90

Trekking in Crinolines

How They Survived

"I'll make it. . . or die trying!"
Whereas societies on every continent and in every epoch have supported the ambitions of men, encouraging their desire to travel and their hunger for fame, the same societies rarely encourage women who seek to perform great deeds.

Of all the fervent dreamers who took the risk of leaving home, country, and continent, of surpassing all known limits and heading further, alone, into uncharted territory, history has recorded only those who survived—and returned. Success: that is what distinguishes great women explorers from the dilettantes and the foolhardy, as far as posterity is concerned. Women who decide to head to the ends of the earth are allowed no margin of error. They must succeed. Or die trying.

"These crinoline trailblazers were witty"

Alexandra Lapierre

What did they harbor, deep within themselves, that guaranteed they would make it? What did they have that allowed them to conquer and survive?

Most of them had nothing. Neither financial resources, nor physical training, nor scientific knowledge. Not even youthfulness. "They must be mad!" thought people at the time.

Mad? Really? There was nothing outlandish about the life they chose. No likelihood of finding *luxe, calme et volupté* (exotic luxuriance, peace, and pleasure). On the contrary, rigor and iron discipline were required. Putting together an expedition calls for a good deal of organization and planning—the difficulties are insurmountable for anyone without a good sense of logistics.

Indeed, it was important to be prepared. To take along weapons, supplies, tools, and medicine. To be familiar with the geography, like May French-Sheldon, before plunging into the African bush. To learn the languages—Persian and Arabic—before disappearing in the Libyan desert, like Alexine Tinne. But what good are all this knowledge and reasoning when faced with the vagaries of chance, the unexpected, the unpredictable? Ultimately it was these women's shrewdness, imagination, and creativity that would see them through. It was their resourcefulness that saved them. Three constant traits, then: inventiveness, level-headedness, stamina.

While these character traits enabled women explorers to survive, there is another, more paradoxical trait that was also typical: a sense of humor. On reading the accounts of the very austere, serious, and devoted Mary Kingsley, what strikes us is her laughter. As does the humor of Isabella Bird, Mary Seacole, and Marianne North. How caustic they could be when picturing themselves, how they mocked themselves.

These crinoline trailblazers were witty. Certain that no situation was ever completely hopeless, they remained phlegmatic and upbeat.

Making their way through the poorest of peoples, amid illness and wretchedness, some women felt compassion. Others, such as Ida Pfeiffer, would remain unmoved, feeling nothing. Whatever their degree of human warmth or egotism, they coped with everything, learning to exist harmoniously with the elements, environments, and lifestyles they encountered, blending into the landscape. All were chameleons, endowed with an exceptional ability to adapt.

Among the tough, frugal, and corseted travelers of the Victorian era were two women who stood apart because of their wealth and their vivacity—two great explorers whose memory has been betrayed or forgotten. The first because her quest failed, her expedition having ended in a bloodbath; the second because she succeeded too quickly, too well, her exploit being too "tongue-in-cheek" to thrill the masses. Such versions of their treks are deceptive, a mere façade, but history would fall for that façade in both instances, recording only a tragic death in the first case, and only boldness, flippancy, and luck in the other.

The first woman was a splendid Dutch aristocrat, Alexine Tinne, who set off to discover the sources of the Nile. The desert people called her "the Blond Sultaness." The second explorer, from South America, was May French-Sheldon, who took the amazing gamble that Masai warriors in Kenya—who were as dangerous as they were inapproachable—would not kill her on sight. On the contrary, she was convinced they would welcome her like a queen. The Africans called her Bébé Bwana (woman master) and even "White Queen."

The only thing their respective voyages have in common is history's subsequent condescension and oversight. And yet. . . .

And yet anyone who takes a good look at the dates of their expeditions and the distances they covered will be amazed by the scope of their accomplishments. Anyone who notes their perseverance, meticulousness, and integrity when dealing with locals can only conclude that their rivals were dishonest and their colleagues were blind.

Even under harsh conditions, they retained such self-respect—respect for what they owed themselves and the men serving them—that no native would ever see them waver, weaken, shiver, perspire, or stumble. Their sense of honor forced them to always appear well groomed before their guides, porters, and camel-handlers—always in hat, boots, and buttons.

In the heart of a desert or savanna they always took their comforts and regalia—they took baths in copper tubs, and took tea at five p.m., changing their clothes, putting on scent, dressing up. They might sup alone, in evening dress, while all around them camels brayed and hippopotamuses bellowed.

So perhaps they were too flamboyant, too *feminine* to be great explorers? Fiddlesticks! They were war chieftains: observing rigid protocol was neither vain nor coquettish. Each ritual they performed was premeditated. The unpacking and repacking of crystal glasses at every halt, the lace tablecloths spread on the sand or in the mud, the silverware, porcelain, the palanquin, the bathtub, and all this ceremonial had a precise significance that served their purpose. It reinforced their prestige among the locals, it enhanced their dignity, it demonstrated their power, it increased their safety. *That* was the point.

What is so moving about Tinne's tragedy, what is so touching about French-Sheldon's apparent frivolity, lies right there: the nobility and modesty that made them mask their courage under the veil of facility and dilettantism. They had *flair*.

The irony is that this flair would be the undoing of one of them, and the salvation of the other. The Arabs and Tuaregs, dazzled by Tinne's power, mistook the large coolers on her camels' backs for treasure chests; thinking they would reap jewels and gold, rather than fruit and sorbets, they massacred her caravan. The few survivors, a handful of Sudanese slaves whom Tinne had bought and freed, made it to Tripoli where they reported the incident. They said that the Blond Sultaness had emerged calmly from her tent, and went straight to the leader of the attackers. She raised her right hand in a sign of peace—which was cut off by a saber before she was cut down by a bullet. Tinne was left to die there in the sand.

She was only thirty-four. Some members of her aristocratic family were heard to sigh, "We warned her!"

It was precisely because she never wanted to hear this particular comment that May French-Sheldon though it wise not to mention the various sufferings she endured during her voyage. Rather than describe a fall into a rock-strewn torrent that left her face, legs, and arms cut and bleeding, or the torture caused by a smashed backbone in the middle of the bush hundreds of miles from Mombasa, she decided to recount only how the Masai marveled every time she appeared before them.

With the hair of her long, blond wig flowing down her back, with her jewelry, daggers, trumpets, and drums, it is easy to see how she made such an impression on men who had never seen a white woman. Although she used all kinds of tricks and artifices to dazzle chiefs and fascinate warriors, French-Sheldon never cheated: between her and them, the seduction was mutual. Over half a century before the rage for African art, she enthusiastically collected jewelry, weapons, masks, and pottery. French-Sheldon was the first woman to take an interest in African culture, the first to recognize its beauty.

The luxuries of her campsites, complete with bathtub and palanquin, prefigure not only the pomp of Vailima, the palace built by Fanny Stevenson on the Samoan Islands, but also the comfort of Karen Blixen's African farm with its piano, vases, crystal, Danish chests, leather-bound books, cases of champagne, gramophone, and records. Able to hack their way through a jungle and also to dance a waltz, these grand ladies rejected neither the society from which they came, nor the worlds they came to discover. Existing in parallel universes, they attempted to reconcile their past with other cultures, refusing to abandon one or the other.

They refused to abandon anything.

A. L.

The Blessings of a Good Thick Skirt

Here we have a new kind of adventuress: the Traveler. Neither courtesan, nor buccaneer, nor freak. In 1850, the Lady Traveler was a title that would take a long time to win its letters of nobility. There were so many things to prove: that a lady could walk barefoot through the jungle of Borneo and still be a lady; that she could handle a theodolite[1] and calculate her position accurately; that she could emerge victorious (in her own, gentle way) from encounters with cannibals and desperadoes. And above all, that she could travel unchaperoned and still retain her virtue. In short, the Traveler would put all her heart and strength into demonstrating that she was not just a lady but also, indeed, "genteel."

Corset drawn tight, dark skirt cut long, hair drawn in a bun beneath hat or modest bonnet: the Lady Traveler's dress was her armor and her banner. It proclaimed that she was exploring new frontiers for science, not love. Vigilance on this point could be extreme—Isabella Bird once demanded that her publisher challenge to a dual a journalist who wrote that she had ridden a horse in trousers.

And was Mary Kingsley to be taken at her word when she asserted to all and sundry that nothing was so suited to African exploration as "a good thick skirt"? Not necessarily, but she was right to state it all the same, because comments like this opened to women explorers the previously hermetically closed doors of the Geographical Societies in Paris and London. Some people may find the travelers of the 1880s unattractive, but deep down they were a fount of passion, intelligence, and often humor.

"Nothing was so suited to African exploration as a good thick skirt"

Mary Kingsley

Alone with her Malay guide,
carrying a miniscule amount
of baggage, Ida Pfeiffer
dove into the equatorial forest
of Borneo. She was the first
Western woman to enter these
unexplored regions.
The sweltering heat, vegetation,
and mud were such that she
was obliged, for the first time
in her long traveling career, to don
trousers underneath her skirt.
She then hiked up folds of cloth
and knotted them around her
waist to make walking easier
as she trudged along the native path.

Ida Pfeiffer

A Little Lady Among Cannibals

Suddenly, at the end of the trail, she spotted a village. It was inhabited by Dayaks, she knew, a tribe of "headhunters." So what did Frau Pfeiffer do? Did she reach for a weapon? Hardly—she never carried one. Did she compose a speech of peace and friendship? No, she wasn't interested in peace and wasn't looking for friends. The only preparations she made for meeting the Borneo headhunters was to put her skirt and petticoats back in place. It would have been unthinkable to encounter a man—any man—dressed in trousers.

This anecdote alone sums up the personality of the first great female explorer in history: bravery in the face of everything, an equally unassailable modesty, and rather limited resources, all of which would contribute to her success. But the anecdote also explains why Pfeiffer has been forgotten for so long. Far from the eccentric Romanticism of the great ladies who traveled the planet's highways and byways, this queen of travel remained a somewhat crabbed middle-class mother despite her extraordinary exploits.

Born in 1797, Ida-Laure Reyer was raised by her beloved father according to rather original principles of education that combined freedom with austerity. Frau Reyer was very disapproving of her husband's methods, and so was determined to correct them once she was widowed. Thus began a painful period for Ida, who claimed in her memoirs that she would burn her own fingertips to escape piano lessons. It took all the diplomacy of an intelligent tutor to finally tame the rebel. He transformed her "from a wild hoydenish creature into a modest girl," she wrote with a certain nostalgia. Frau Reyer would nevertheless soon regret her choice of tutor; apparently she never anticipated that the "modest girl" and her Pygmalion would

fall in love. But fall in love they did, which triggered a new rebellion, new struggle, and new defeat for Ida. The tutor, of far too humble background, was dismissed and the young lady was shut away.

Her will broken, Ida agreed to marry Herr Doktor Pfeiffer. She meekly assumed the role of submissive wife and loving mother, a role she played for twenty-seven years. Without complaint, without melancholy, without anger. No one at the time could have imagined the dreams churning beneath her bonnet. Yet she would later say that, during all that time, she hoped one day to live out her dream. Her children grew up, married, moved out. Ida began studying geography in secret. When the time finally came to break her chains, she was already forty-seven years old. Prudently, she informed her family that she intended to visit an acquaintance who was living in Constantinople. "Folly!" replied her sons, convinced that she would return in a matter a weeks, having overtaxed her slim income and her equally slim frame. They were unaware that she intended to travel right around the world. And they were incredulous when they discovered that she had actually done it. What's more, she then took

a second trip around the world. The only thing that brought a halt to Ida Pfeiffer's globe-trotting was her death, fifteen years later.

Brazil, China, Singapore, Ceylon, India, Mesopotamia, Persia, Kurdistan, Polynesia, Borneo, Madagascar—Frau Pfeiffer saw no reason why she should ever set her scant luggage down. Her taste for travel remained strong and her techniques were tried and tested. She didn't have money, but didn't need any. She only embarked on ships that offered her a free berth—on deck, if necessary. If there were no inn, she was happy with a straw mat in a caravanserai, a barn, or a porch. If the company were too unsavory for her taste, she would insist that the ship's captain or caravanserai owner find her some-place suited to her sex and her dignity. Her motto might have been, "See as much as possible, spend as little as possible." She ate little, and anyway might similarly insist—she never begged—that her host supply her with board as well as bed. Woe betide the thoughtless ones who refused. They were explicitly identified and harshly treated in the accounts she published at every return, to growing critical esteem. "I always succeeded in carrying out my own will," she wrote,

Pages 30 and 31: A lemur; and a portrait of Ida Pfeiffer in the forest, based on a photograph.

Facing page: Ida Pfeiffer's expedition encountered wild animals and occasionally hostile peoples (in Brazil, far left) but was also received by royal courts (in India).

Above: "I was advised to wrap myself in a large cloth and wear a veil when I went out." (Ida Pfeiffer, *A Lady's Voyage Round the World*, 1888).

Above: Ida Pfeiffer received at the Malagasy court.

Facing page: Geysers in Iceland as depicted in one of Pfeiffer's books in 1852.

"I found that energy and boldness have a weight with all people, whether Arabs, Persians, Bedouins, or others."

Only another woman might topple such haughtiness. It took the queen of Madagascar, Ranavalona, to get the better of our Viennese conqueror. With contempt and violence the queen expelled the upstart who had the carelessness, for the first time in her traveling career, to become involved in a palace conspiracy.[1] Pfeiffer never recovered from that voyage. Rather than the humiliation, however, it was the so-called "Madagascar fever" that felled her. Shortly after her return to Vienna she died from complications caused by her illness, on October 28, 1858.

This portrait of Frau Pfeiffer might make us smile, and yet we would be mistaken to mock her. Her viewpoint, if somewhat narrow, was nevertheless sharp. Thus she noted, among other things, that the condition of women in lands then dubbed "primitive" was not so dreadful as claimed. Working women in Vienna, she said, were treated much worse. "There is no fate more wretched than that of a poor woman in Europe." Honesty and common sense thus largely made up for Pfeiffer's prejudices and quaint bonnets. Colette, a French novelist as sensual as Pfeiffer was puritanical, knew what she was talking about when she wrote to a friend in 1944, "Have you read Ida Pfeiffer's travel journals? Marvelous!"

A moral lesson in a remote village in Kurdistan

They were not deficient in good nature, and when I noticed anything amiss in their behavior they were very willing to acknowledge themselves in the wrong. A little girl of seven years old, for instance, named Ascha, was particularly naughty. The moment anything was refused her, she would fling herself on the ground, howl with all her might, and even roll herself purposely in the dirt. . . . I tried to make her understand the impropriety of this proceeding, and I succeeded beyond my expectations. I endeavored in the same manner to give [the child] a little instruction in cleanliness, and very soon it would go and give itself a good washing, and then come jumping to show me its hands and face.

No less fortunate was I with the women; I used to point to their torn clothes, and then fetch needle and thread, and show them how they might be mended. They were quite pleased with the discovery, and very soon I had quite a sewing school around me.

Ida Pfeiffer, *A Lady's Voyage Round the World*, translated from the German by Mrs. Percy Sinnett [1851] (London: Century, 1988).

A large steamship slowly headed up the Nile. Its waterline was low, indicating that it was heavily laden. A throng of servants and sailors rushed around the deck. In the middle of all this agitation, indifferent to the sensation they were causing, sat four women. Nestling in the blossoming folds of their white skirts, they sat upright, corseted, hair rolled into a bun beneath a brimmed hat or a bonnet discreetly trimmed with lace. What were they doing as the shoreline of the vast Sudanese desert slipped by? They were doing needlework.

Alexine Tinne

Tragedy at the Source of the Nile

"They must be demented!" exclaimed a giant, bearded man on learning that the ship, hired at great cost, had sailed.

His indignation was triggered not by the women's silly on-board occupation nor by the unreasonable amount of luggage they had stowed.

"They really must be mad," he repeated. "A young woman alone with the Dinka tribe? All the natives are as naked as the day they were born!"

In short, this comment by the explorer Samuel White Baker, who jotted it down in a letter when he reached Khartoum shortly after Alexine Tinne's expedition had set out, explains why it was so difficult for a woman to be an explorer in 1860. Not because she was a fragile creature; Baker, like all travelers in his day, realized that mothers and wives were able to cope with the toughest conditions. It was difficult because modesty could not cope with what the body could handle. Or rather, *should* not cope. If she were willing, with no fear for her modesty, to share the life of naked men, a woman was no longer a lady but an "adventuress," hence a suspect individual.

Yet those women embroidering quietly on deck were indeed true ladies, indeed grand ladies.

Alexine Tinne was born in 1835 into one of Holland's most noble families, the Van Cappellens. Close to the royal family, it boasted a vast fortune and connections in every European capital. Ever since birth, Alexine knew what travel meant; she and her mother belonged to that set of cosmopolitan aristocrats whose only boundaries were social. From princely courts to fashionable spas, they never spent more than a few months in one place. Harriet Tinne never asked

CAIRO - *General View*

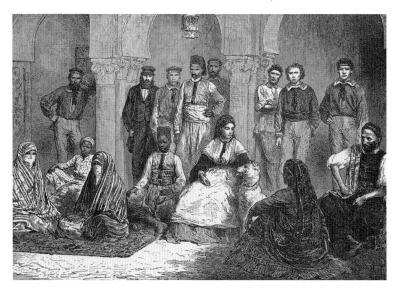

herself whether her daughter liked such a life, for she could imagine no other. Yet once Alexine had reached her nineteenth birthday, in 1854, her mother acknowledged the need to return to The Hague—the time had come to put the young woman on the market for a husband. Alexine played along, at least for one season of balls and receptions. She accepted all invitations, gracefully received all compliments—but rejected every suitor. Then she repacked her trunks. But now it was Alexine who led her mother in her wake. In 1856, the two women found themselves in Egypt. It was their first visit to the Orient; they hired a boat to sail up the Nile, and went from monument to monument at a time when this kind of cruise was still an adventure.

Thrilled and delighted, the sixty-three-year-old Harriet would have been satisfied with this exploit, one that would make her a celebrity within the salons of The Hague. But Alexine was spurred by a desire that a Romantic, Oriental voyage could not fulfill. Educated and inquiring, she was interested in the great geographic debate of the day: where was the source of the Nile? Two years earlier, the explorer John H. Speke claimed to have located it at the mouth of a large lake; but his incautious claims were challenged by Richard Burton, an old Africa hand. Speke would therefore have to retrace his route and bring back proof of his discovery. The lack of certainty left a gap into which a dream could still fit. So Alexine dreamed, and her mother let her dream on. Even when Alexine began spreading maps on the Oriental carpets brought back from Cairo, Harriet raised no objection.

Egypte

In 1860, Alexine set off again. With her mother, once again—the pair were inseparable. This time, they said to themselves, they would go beyond the temples, they would go as far as the source of the Nile. Alexine had everything required for success: intelligence, determination, and wealth. Intelligent, she was able to organize an expedition, command a troop of one hundred men, and learn geography and topography (she already spoke several languages, including Arabic). Determined, she was able to quell a mutiny on her own, to negotiate on equal terms with a hostile chieftain, and to face up to the worst slave traffickers. Wealthy, she had her own fortune. But that would be her downfall.

A nomad all her life, Alexine knew how to travel. But as a magnificent aristocrat, she always took her own world with her when she traveled. Why should she leave it behind this time? The contents of her baggage made Baker shudder as he watched the expedition pass by—and he was right: thirty-six trunks divided between three boats, plus tents, camp beds, sheets, blankets—all quite reasonable, so far—but then a tea service in Chinese porcelain, a canteen of silver cutlery, an entire library, hat boxes, parasols, a camera complete with developing apparatus, an easel, canvases, pigments, and so on.

Nor were the traveling companions selected with any greater discernment. Apart from the myriad servants, Alexine took along her mother, Harriet, her mother's chambermaid, Anna, and her own chambermaid, Flora. The three other women were as courageous as the leader of the expedition, but less obsessed with finding the

Pages 36 and 37: Mashra ur-Raqq, Sudan; Tinne on her mount.

Facing page: View of Cairo; and Tinne in her house in Algiers.

Above: A lively street in Cairo.

Above: Portrait of Alexine Tinne in Egypt; an engraving showing the marshland of Bahr el-Ghazal.

Facing page: Contemporary maps of the regions visited by Tinne.

source of the Nile. They went along because they couldn't imagine refusing their darling whatever she asked of them.

On May 11, 1862, the expedition left Khartoum. On September 30, it reached Gondokoro, the southernmost navigable point. There they were halted by slave traders. It proved impossible to find porters and supplies. Alexine didn't seem to realize that the very size of her expedition was the obstacle. Rather than give up, she changed destination. She would steam up the Bahr el-Ghazal as far as the legendary land of the Nyam-Nyams (Azande), then head overland for the Atlantic Ocean, if possible. Thus her steamship headed into a swamp the size of a whole country, advancing just a few miles per day. Then they set out across dry land with forty mules and four camels. In the spring of 1863 the expedition was obliged to halt and wait out the rainy season—they were stalled for several months by non-stop rain. To pass the time, the ladies did needlework, read, or gathered botanical samples. Neither the rain, nor the mud, nor the insects, not even sores that never healed and outbreaks of malarial fever, could dampen their spirits. Thus, when Harriet stayed in bed one morning, Alexine wasn't overly worried. Rest and quinine was a well-known remedy—the only remedy, for that matter, in those days. This time, however, Harriet never got out of bed. She died on July 22, 1863, and was followed shortly by Flora, and then Anna. In the

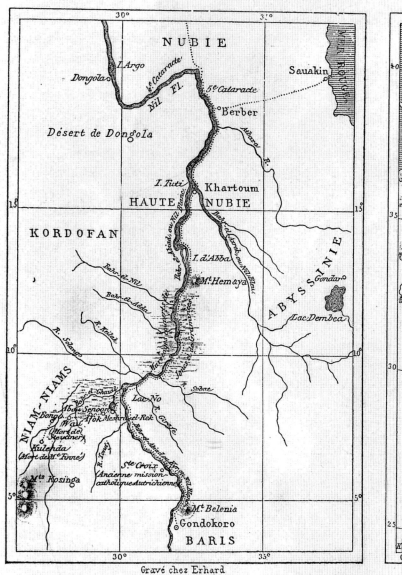

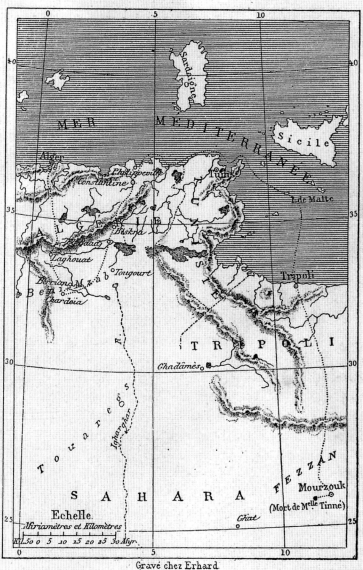

first letter she was able to dispatch to her family, Alexine wrote, almost incredulous: "They've all departed."

Alexine never reached the Atlantic. Her mother having died, she could not imagine going on. Perhaps this is the way in which she differed from her male counterparts. Livingstone, after the death of his wife in similar conditions, didn't even pause to wonder. He carried on and completed his exploration of the Zambezi. But Alexine headed back in January 1864, once the rains had ended, accompanied by three coffins.

She would never return to The Hague, however. Far from having assuaged her passion for travel, the tragedy exacerbated it. She had traveled in order to explore, but now she would travel to flee, in a suicidal rage. Four years were spent on an endless cruise among Mediterranean ports. "I like this life," she claimed in 1869, "I want to sail forever." Yet soon afterward she abandoned her yacht in order to cross the Sahara on camelback.

Above: The tragic death of Alexine Tinne.

Facing page: Cairo and its feluccas.

It was in Tripoli that she caught the Africa bug again. This time, she wanted to reach the Sultanate of Bornu, beyond Lake Chad. Once again, she hoped to reach the Atlantic, but this time she organized an expedition that was too big, too lavish, and too conspicuous to avoid running into trouble. This came after two months on the trail, near the cliffs of Jabal al-Sawda. A Tuareg chieftain, Bu Bekker, caught sight of the caravan of two hundred people and several tons of equipment when it was camped under the protection of Ikhenukhen, chieftain of the Ajjer. Bu Bekker and his men caught up with the "Blond Sultaness" in the oasis of Wadi Aberdjoush. A quarrel immediately broke out between his warriors and the guide appointed by Ikhenukhen; a servant tried to intervene, but was impaled on a lance. Alexine, alerted by the ruckus, came out of her tent. A survivor said he saw her raise her hand in a gesture of appeasement, but one of the Tuaregs slashed her forearm with a sword; then a shot rang out, and she fell. Killing and pillaging then ensued, with such success that nothing was ever found of the treasures traveling with the foreign woman—nor her body. From her numerous entourage only a few Sudanese slaves survived, whom she had saved from Gondokoro slave traders and then freed. They made their way to Tripoli and recounted the murder to the authorities.

CAIRO - River Nile.
74

*G*ifts for the Sultan

When preparing her expedition across the Sahara, Alexine wrote to a friend to go to Paris or Brussels to buy some objects typical of Europe of the day. They were presents to be offered to the sultan of Bornu when she finally met up with him. None of these objects was found after her death. Here is the list she appended to her letter.

"A microscope, not a very dear one, but good enough to astonish a person who has never seen one;

– two ice machines and powder to make it. . . .
– a sewing machine of a simple kind . . . .
– a *reveille matin* or clock. . . . Some, I am told, light a candle at the moment they wake one;
– eight pieces of silk of bright and gaudy colors. . . .
– some bottles of *encre sympathique* [invisible ink]. . . .
– some magnifying glasses—six of these will suffice;
– an *appareil photographique* Debroni if its price does not exceed 100 francs. . . .

– a looking glass with a gaudily guilt [*sic*] frame. . . .
– twenty-five yards of fine scarlet cloth; four pieces of red and yellow velvet. . . .
– a chest of good green tea;
– some bonbons of sorts in about twenty of those gaudy things the French give to children on New Year's day;
– twenty-four gaudy cotton handkerchiefs; twenty-four gaudy silk handkerchiefs."

Penelope Gladstone, *Travels of Alexine* (London: John Murray, 1970).

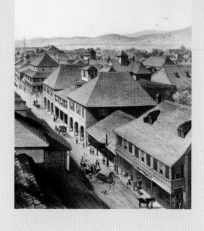

*S*wift-footed Hermes
is the god of merchants
and travelers. He may well have
been Mary Seacole's very special
patron, since the heart of this
jovial Caribbean woman, who
became a celebrity in the London
of the 1850s, was torn between
two loves—business and travel.
The first love of Miss Mary
Grant, as she was then known,
was for trade in fine goods,
which she owed to her family
background. Her mother
ran a comfortable hotel
in Kingston, Jamaica, which Mary
decided to help prosper.

Mary Seacole

The Merchant with a Heart of Gold

With that goal in mind, at age nineteen she made her first ocean crossing to London, taking a cargo of spices, calico prints, and preserves of exotic fruit. She returned with handsome profits and her second lifelong love: for travel. Her appetite for discovery was bottomless, but she didn't have a comfortable income, and she remained a merchant at heart. She therefore employed one enthusiasm to fund the other. She traveled among the large and small islands of the Caribbean, and along the coast of the continent, sometimes taking chests of sharks' teeth, sometimes exotic fruit or old rum. "Thus I spent some time in New Providence, bringing home with me a large collection of handsome shells and rare shell-work, which created quite a sensation," and which thus sold swiftly. Mary spent five years traveling and trading, until she reached the age of twenty-five.

Thanks to the dowry she herself built up, in 1836 Miss Grant married Mr. Seacole, a Jamaican gentleman of not very robust health. They took over the boarding house in Kingston, which is where Mary Seacole spent the next fourteen years. It was not all plain sailing—she became a widow, a fire broke out, and a cholera epidemic struck. But restlessness began to overcome her. What could she do?

Her brother, who had moved to Panama, offered a solution. There was money to made, he said, where he had settled. That was just the excuse she needed, because Mrs. Seacole couldn't imagine traveling just for the fun of it.

Why was there money to be made in the swampy, wooded little country of Panama? It was a question of timing. In 1848, word of the discovery of gold in California spread like wildfire across America

Pages 44 and 45: The trading town of Kingston, Jamaica, in the early 19th century; and a portrait of Mary Seacole.

Above: A street in the port of Kingston; and a painted portrait of the hotel owner.

Facing page: The isthmus of Panama and the surrounding forest (engraving of 1879).

and into Europe. Soon everyone was rushing westward. At that time, the safest way to reach California was still via the isthmus of Panama, because both Cape Horn and the great plains remained dangerous itineraries. Panama thus found itself swelled with travelers seeking to get from one ocean to the other; crowds arrived in ebbs and flows as ships docked and sailed. The land-crossing between Atlantic and Pacific was done via rivers and mud tracks, on mule, which meant sleeping in the "towns" that sprang up like mushrooms (and often returned swiftly to the mud from which they sprang). So it was Cruces, Panama, where Mary Seacole decided to strike it rich in 1850. In a wooden plank hotel with its single dormitory and one meal a day, she welcomed thousands of travelers, few of whom were very demanding.

Easy money? Hardly. The customers of "Mother Seacole" were weary but hardly refined. The planet's direst adventurers found themselves crowded into a camp ringed by forest and epidemics. "It seemed as capital a nursery for ague and fever as Death could hit upon anywhere . . . . When we arrived a steady down-pour of rain was falling from an inky sky; the white man who met us on the wharf appeared ghostly and wraith-like, and the very negroes seemed pale and wan." In a Wild-West ambience, the hotel manager had to stand up to the most aggressive customers and to satisfy all the rest, defending her fragile establishment against floods of mud and swarms of insects. In the end, Seacole did not make the fortune she had hoped to acquire in this rather grim new world. Or at least, she lost her profits very fast. She was advised to invest her profits in a

gold mine at the mouth of a small river in the southern part of the isthmus. After a journey in a small boat down the swampy waters of the Panamanian forests, she arrived at a strange colony run with an iron fist by a man who exploited Indians to dig up the banks of the river in search of gold—which didn't exist. Seacole returned home empty-handed.

It hardly mattered, for in Cruces she discovered a treasure of another kind. Not a trove of money, but one that would earn her fame. Indeed, if Mary Seacole has gone down in history it was not due to her success as a hotel and store manager. It was another, hidden passion—medicine—that would later earn her three medals, including Britain's Crimean Medal and France's Légion d'Honneur. Seacole's love of medicine was not only unsuited to a middle-class woman but was wildly ambitious for a "Creole," yet was understandable since her mother had already been a "doctress" and had spent much time treating the convalescent soldiers who stayed in her boarding house (not to mention Mary's husband, her most docile patient). What sparked Mary's own vocation was an outbreak of cholera. For the people camping at Cruces, as well as for the Indians and wretched folk all around, Seacole would forever be known as the "yellow doctress." From a fine-goods merchant she graduated to nurse, doctor, undertaker—and researcher. Indeed, Seacole did not merely wash bodies and administer calomel, she became interested in exploring the mystery of cholera. She wanted to *know*. So one night, she took the body of an orphaned infant who had just died in her arms and autopsied it

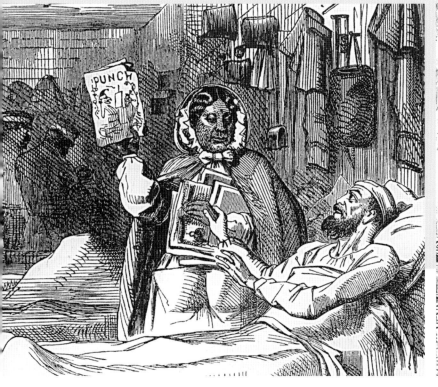

outside town, armed with a scalpel. She hoped to get a better understanding of the disease; at that time, in that place, an autopsy carried out by a woman, by someone who was not a certified doctor, was a sacrilege. Ten years later, when writing her memoirs, Seacole would apologize even as she admitted, "It seems a strange deed to accomplish, and I am sure I could not wield the scalpel or the substitute I then used now, but at that time the excitement had strung my mind up to a high pitch of courage and determination; and perhaps the daily, almost hourly, scenes of death had made me somewhat callous."

We don't know how much the doctress learned from the post-mortem, but it certainly confirmed her true vocation. When war broke out in the Crimea, on the boundary between the Russian and Ottoman empires, British soldiers began dying of typhus and other illnesses due to poor hygiene. When Seacole learned that a brave Englishwoman, Florence Nightingale, had begun organizing the first-ever corps of nurses to go to a battlefront, Seacole felt a great desire stir within her: she would be a nurse in the Crimea. She was sure she would be as welcome as she was needed, because she shrank from neither blood nor filth.

But Seacole overlooked one detail. She was called not just "doctress," but "yellow doctress." She was not completely white. As far as whites were concerned, her swarthy skin negated all the credibility that her reputation might have earned her. When she arrived in London the only thing the proper-thinking ladies around Miss Nightingale could see was the color of Seacole's skin. Even though she was wearing a fine dress of canary-yellow satin and a flowery hat, the "nurses" wouldn't even look at her. Her skills were not enough—in order to be accepted as one of Miss Nightingale's nurses, a high-society pedigree was essential

As a true trailblazer, however, Seacole was not about to give up. She would not let a few stiff-necked, thin-lipped ladies get in her way. If she couldn't be a nurse on the Crimean front, she would open an officer's mess there. She sent an announcement to all her military acquaintances—of whom she had many, thanks to the family boarding house: "Mrs. Mary Seacole (late of Kingston, Jamaica), respectfully announces to her former kind friends . . . . that she has taken her passage in the screw-steamer *Hollander* . . . . intending on her arrival at Balaclava to establish a mess table and comfortable quarters for sick and convalescent officers."

It was a brilliant idea. Miss Nightingale had not taken the risk of going quite so near the front. Her hospital was established a safe distance away, on the island of Scutari. Seacole, meanwhile, was so close to the fighting that soldiers naturally found their way to her establishment. It was a god send, for it offered everything: food, tobacco, medication, beds, and the soothing hands of the doctress, as

Facing page: Mary Seacole is caricatured in the press; an engraving of her hospice in the Crimea.

Above: A nurse aiding a wounded soldier in the Crimea, 1855.

Above: General Sir George Brown and two of his men in the Crimea; the port of Balaklava.

Facing page: *The Wonderful Adventures of Mrs. Seacole*, 1857.

ready to prepare a soup as to lance a whitlow. Mud, blood, and fever obscured the color of Seacole's skin—all the soldiers noticed was her smile, her laughter, her jokes, her ribbons, and her flowers. Her Majesty's officers would never forget her, nor would they fail to show their gratitude.

Back in London after victory in 1856, when the officers learned that Mother Seacole had gone bankrupt by feeding and caring for them rather than attending to her account books, they organized a subscription and a gala event in her honor. The Jamaican healer, that gold-seeking, yellow-skinned Creole with flashy skirts, was carried in triumph on the shoulders of her former patients and customers. She wept with joy—and went on to enjoy a happy ending. Mary Seacole died peacefully and comfortably in 1881, coddled by all the good families of London whose sons she had saved. The god Hermes had obviously kept efficient watch over her.

Mary Seacole, age sixteen

As I grew into womanhood, I began to indulge in that longing to travel which will never leave me while I have health and vigor.

I. . . . never followed with my gaze the stately ships bound [for Europe] without longing to be in them, and to see the blue hills of Jamaica fade into the distance.

Mary Seacole,
The Wonderful Adventures of Mary Seacole in Many Lands, (New York: Oxford University Press, 1990)

Readers may recall the comment made by the explorer Samuel White Baker as he watched Alexine Tinne's expedition sail up the Nile: "They must be demented." Given that it was uttered by a nineteenth-century male, this exclamation might be expected, even understandable. But it wasn't. It was an inexcusable comment because on that very day, standing next to Baker and watching the same spectacle, was a young woman barely twenty years old, whom he was planning to take deeper into Africa than Tinne would ever go.

Above: Watercolor by Samuel Baker
of a butchered hippopotamus.

Facing page: Samuel and Florence Baker wearing
explorers' clothing, from the frontispiece
of *The Albert N'Yanza*

was knighted, and she was received by the best families of England,
including the prince of Wales. Samuel even tried to have her
presented to the queen, but this campaign resulted in his only
setback: Victoria, after making inquiries that implied that young
woman just might have been "intimate" with her husband prior to
marriage, refused to meet her.

Florence may well have tired of the constraints of good
Victorian society, for when Samuel accepted a mission proposed by
the khedive of Egypt to eliminate the slave trade in the Upper Nile
regions, Florence immediately volunteered to depart anew. Thus she
spent three more years in Africa, from February 1870 to April 1873,
accompanying the small army launched in pursuit of the slavers. But
that mission was truly impossible, for the ruler who instigated it was
himself involved in the crime he charged Samuel Baker with
punishing. The expedition ended in a deadly ambush followed by a
headlong flight across the savanna, during which Florence never lost
the cool head she kept throughout her life. She spent spare moments
mending the couple's clothes, making preserves, serving tea, or
cooking a "not very young" hippopotamus steak. And when the situation called for it, she could do more. "We found Florence in a
capital state of preparation," recounted a member of the expedition
on returning from a reconnaissance with Samuel. "She had posted
double sentries all round, got all the guns ready, and was prepared
for action."

It was nevertheless the exploring couple's last adventure.
Samuel was fifty-two at the time. When he died in his wife's arms

was constantly amazed. When commenting on the entry of an intruder into their tent in the middle of night, he wrote, "A slight pull at my sleeve showed me that my wife, too, had noticed the [intruder], as this was always the signal she made if anything occurred at night that required vigilance. Possessing a share of *sangfroid* admirably adapted to African travel, Mrs. Baker was not a screamer, and never even whispered in the moment of danger—a touch of my sleeve was considered a sufficient warning."

One detail worth noting is that Florence, unlike her counterparts, did not hesitate to swap her skirts for trousers during the long months of trek—probably because she was less concerned than the others to present herself as a "gentlewoman" (at least during that period of her life). It is this kind of detail that helps us to assess the hypocrisy of ladies who claimed long and loud that nothing was more practical for crossing mountains and deserts than "a good thick skirt."

Although Samuel Baker was highly discreet about Florence's presence in Khartoum, he subsequently made up for it. He would constantly mention her in his letters, books, and even in his talks before the learned scholars of the Royal Geographical Society. The young Hungarian slave was thus thrust into another kind of adventure. Florence didn't care about whether or not she passed for a "gentlewoman" in the middle of an African village in Buganda—she had already come a long way, and would go much further still—but in London she had to learn to adopt the crinolines of a true lady. Indeed, she became Lady Baker with a capital L once her husband

Pages 52 and 53: English explorer John H. Speke seeking the sources of the Nile, followed by Kamrasi's satanic escort; and Florence Baker in the desert (Samuel Baker, *The Nile Tributaries of Abyssinia*, 1867).

Facing page, top: Samuel and Florence Baker host English explorers John H. Speke and James Augustus Grant on board their boat on the Upper Nile in 1861 (engraving of 1880). Facing page, bottom: Florence and Samuel Baker arrive in a hostile village during their voyage to the source of the Nile from 1861 to 1864 (engraving of 1880).

Above: An engraving from Samuel W. Baker's *The Albert N'Yanza: Great Basin of the Nile*, 1870.

their letters and accounts, neither Speke nor Grant mentioned their colleague's pretty mistress, providing supplementary proof that Baker still wished that no one in England know he was being accompanied. Perhaps he was still not sure of his feelings in that month of April 1861. But he was apparently sure three years later, when he and Florence returned to Khartoum side by side. The first thing he did on returning to London was to marry the young Hungarian slave, even before he went to the Royal Geographical Society. From that day onward, until his dying breath in 1893, he insisted that Florence was the love of his life.

What did they do between 1861 and 1865? They spent thirty months trekking, camping, and exploring a region ravaged by traders in slaves and ivory. Together, Samuel and Florence crossed the unstable kingdoms of Bunyoro and Buganda (in today's Uganda). Together, they faced a mutiny, scarcity of food, rainy seasons, and attacks of fever. Together, they lived among allegedly unpredictable tribes such as the Nuer, the Shilluk, and the Acholi, winning those peoples' esteem. Together, barely able to stand, the Bakers were the first Europeans to set eyes on what they would name Lake Albert and the Murchison Falls, thereby completely solving the enigma of the source of the Nile.

During this adventure—one of the finest in the history of exploration—Florence showed herself to be much more than a concubine brought along for fun. Day after day, the twenty-year-old woman proved that she could deal with the direst situations with a calm and determination that many men would fail to match. Samuel

Florence Baker

The Hungarian Slave

Baker had a good reason for failing to mention the presence of this person in Khartoum. She was not his wife, nor was his family aware of her existence (Baker was a widower, the father of four children). Worse, Florence Finnian von Sass wasn't even English. Of Hungarian stock, she had no family and no home country. Baker met her in Moldavia in 1858 during a hunting expedition. Florence was vague about her origins, and the subject would long remain taboo among Baker descendents. According to the official version, her parents were massacred during the Hungarian revolution of 1848, but the little girl managed to flee, thanks to her nanny, to the fringes of the Ottoman Empire, where she was taken in by the community of aristocratic refugees until she met Baker. According to another version, advanced by more recent biographers, little Florence was allegedly sold to a Turkish lord, and was being sold on the white slave market when the English explorer saw her—and bought her.[1] The only certainty is that she was aged seventeen when they met.

The couple was thus in Khartoum three years later, watching the boats sail up the Nile. Baker was preparing a major project. An adventurer by trade and by temperament, he intended to take part in the race to find the source of the Nile, a quest then at its height. While he was readying his departure, however, the explorers John H. Speke and James Grant beat him to it; the two men had just discovered the Ripon Falls, on the edge of Lake Victoria, from which the Nile flowed. So was the enigma totally resolved? Speke, playing the perfect gentleman, admitted to Baker that he had not be able to follow the Nile along its entire course between Lake Victoria and Gondokoro—the map still contained a vast blank that had to be filled in order to provide absolute confirmation of the source. In

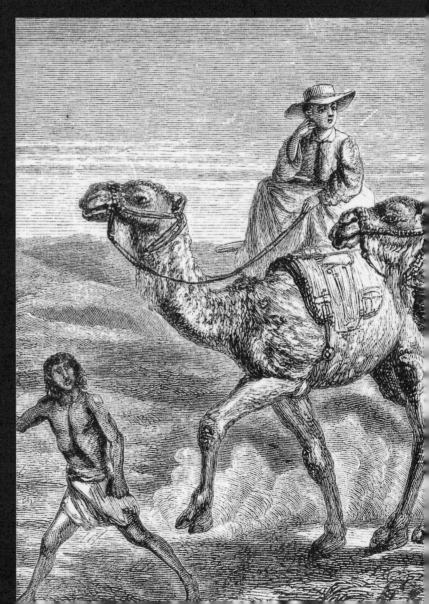

twenty years later, on December 30, 1893, he whispered, "Flooey, Flooey, how can I leave you?"

"Flooey" lived for more than another twenty years, until 1916. She was highly popular and sought after, and lived in a fine English manor full of children (her husband's descendents), preserves, and flowers. She reigned there as a charming grandmother in a black velvet dress. How many of her guests in the early twentieth century realized that the old lady dressed in mourning was still famous and celebrated in distant Ugandan villages, known by the name of Anyadue, "Daughter of the Moon"? Yet that is precisely what was noted by two travelers to the region, the first of whom passed through in 1899, the second in 1950.[2]

Letter from Samuel to his sister, Ellen, May 20, 1873

For 130 miles she marched on foot. . . . sometimes marching 16 miles in one stretch through gigantic grasses and tangled forests. She was always close behind me carrying ammunition in the midst of constant fighting—lances sometimes almost grazing her—one of her servant boys killed near her— the horse-keepers and horse killed just before her. Seven days consecutively we fought during the march against the whole country organized in ambuscades in the terrible grasses in which an elephant would be invisible. My only fear was for her. At night a bundle of damp grass was the only bed— no food beside sweet potatoes and plantains. . . . Through all these trials she has, thank God, been unscathed either by sickness or accident and she has always been my little Prime Minister to give good counsel in moments of difficulty or danger.

Anne Baker, *Morning Star*
(London: William Kimber, 1972).

Isabella Bird was a sickly
young woman who lived on
potions and sofas in the gray
light of a Scottish parsonage.
Tortured by a painful back
that left her no respite,
her only family was her beloved
and devoted sister, Henrietta.
Her sorrowful temperament
discouraged suitors, so that
she was already forty years old
when a doctor somewhat
shrewder than the rest
recommended that
she take a long voyage.

Isabella Bird

For the Love of a Desperado

"Why not?" she said to herself on hearing the strange prescription.

So she packed her bags and set off one summer's day in 1872. For the first six months, she wasn't convinced it was a good idea. The cruise to Australia was grim and she was in constant pain. She was advised to sail on to California, where the climate was reputed to be good for invalids. The only ship she could find was an old paddle steamer. "It hardly matters," she said to herself, for she had lost all taste for life. "It hardy matters," she repeated when a hurricane appeared on the Pacific horizon.

But then a miracle occurred. While the hull of the ship creaked and cracked under the hurricane's hellish wind, while passengers and crew were commending their souls to God, Isabella was reborn. "It is so like living in a new world," she wrote to her sister Henrietta that same evening, "so free, so fresh, so vital, so careless, so unfettered, so full of interest that one grudges being asleep." By braving the fury of the elements, acting boldly, and thriving on danger, Bird finally found her own path.

Full of new vigor, she made a long sojourn in the Sandwich Islands (modern Hawaii). And another miracle occurred: after the thrill of the sea, Bird discovered the thrill of riding. She had thought herself unable to remain on a horse, because her back pain prevented her from riding sidesaddle; but Hawaiian women, she noted, sat astride the saddle. Not in trousers, of course, which was unthinkably indecent to Bird's mind, but in voluminous skirts stitched in such as way as to make it impossible to see that they were, in fact, culottes. Bird observed, studied, and tried. It was a revelation. She immediately had a pair of "bloomers" made for herself, and would henceforth always pack them in her luggage. And she made

sure they were pictured in her book to prove that she remained lady-like in all situations.

In the summer of 1873, Bird reached the coast of California. Now seized with an insatiable appetite for life, she was finally ready for true adventure. Cheerful, witty and well-brought-up, she was appreciated by everyone she met. It was in the Rocky Mountains that she finally had the adventure she sought. Her goal was Estes Park, an isolated valley whose wild grandeur had been described to her. It was inhabited only by a Scottish rancher, a few trappers scattered in the hills, and a desperado. Her first encounter was the outlaw—an unforgettable meeting: "His face was remarkable. He is a man about forty-five, and must have been strikingly handsome." Despite her efforts, the tone of Bird's letters allowed her sister Henrietta to perceive the fascination that Jim Nugent held for a sensitive woman who knew so little of love. Far from being a vulgar bandit, the "desperado" turned out to be as cultivated as he was handsome, as courteous as he was well-built. As to the rumors of his past crimes, they merely made him more attractive.

As little as Bird may have expected herself to fall in love with an outlaw who dressed in wolf skins, she expected even less that he might fall in love with her. For she didn't realize that she was attractive in addition to being intelligent. Not even a typhoon the Pacific could compare with the tempest that gripped her when Nugent declared his love for her two months later.

Yet she had sensed she was in danger of falling in love. That is why, after spending just a few weeks at the Estes ranch, climbing

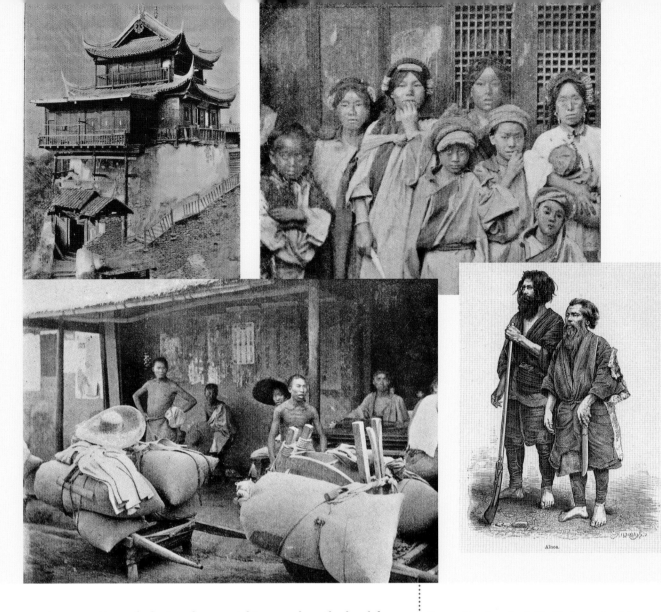

Ainos.

nearby summits, and playing the cowgirl to round up the herd for winter, she headed off to discover the Rockies on her little mare Birdie, riding eight hours a day in all weather, sleeping in log cabins among the trappers.

Eight hundred miles of solitary travel in the snow, with just one blanket and three dresses—of which one was silk—as baggage: Bird didn't intend to return to Estes Park at the conclusion of her escapade. But the money order she was expecting to find in Denver hadn't arrived, so she decided to spend an inexpensive winter among her friends at the Scottish ranch. Her return was a sign from heaven, as far as the artful desperado was concerned; less than a week later he declared that he had loved her at first sight.

As violent as her internal tempest was, Bird never once considered yielding. Her own image of herself prevented her from imagining a life shared with a former criminal, hiding in a cabin, with grizzlies and whisky as sole company. Miss Bird valued her honor as much as her freedom. Thus she left Estes Park after a wrenching encounter that left her in tears, as she admitted in a letter to Henrietta: "My heart dissolved with pity for him and his dark, lost, self-ruined life."

She was back in Scotland by the spring. There she worked on her first travel book. Although still a solitary and virtuous woman, Bird became a professional adventurer. Armed with an inflatable pillow, a mosquito net, a rubber bathtub and three outfits (a tweed suit for the cold, her bloomers for riding, and the inevitable silk dress), she lived with the Ainu tribe on the island of Hokkaido and

Pages 58 and 59: Isabella Bird wearing bloomers, her favorite garment, while holding the reins of her horse; portrait of Isabella Bird.

Facing page: Traditional boat on the Min River, and Bird at her writing desk.

Above, clockwise: Chinese temple at Lifan Ting; a Mantzu family; workers on the Chengdu plain; two Ainu men, who inhabit Japan's northern region.

Above: Bird in travel dress in Armenia; trappers posing with a young Native American in Colorado in 1873.

Facing page: An autographed portrait of Isabella Bird.

she rode an elephant in Malaya. The death of Henrietta would interrupt Isabella's travels. Distressed, the traveler lost her appetite for new horizons. So much so, that she married a Dr. Bishop and settled down forever. Five years later she was a widow. And what else could she do, but set off again?

In 1889, despite her aging bones and white hair, she retrieved her trunk from the attic. Kashmir, Tibet, China, Korea, home again, then off to Morocco. Nothing could stop her, neither blizzards in Kurdistan nor floods in China, nor a broken rib in a stream in Tibet, nor a broken arm in a cart accident in Manchuria, not even a xenophobic riot in China (in which, aged sixty, she was nearly killed). She was about to embark once more for China when she finally took to her bed, immobilized by a tumor and a thrombosis. She died on October 7, 1904, after eighteen months of an illness that, this time, no voyage could cure.

It was Bird's second travel book, *A Lady's Life in the Rocky Mountains,* published in 1879, that recounted her Far West adventures. But readers found no trace of her feelings for Jim Nugent in it, just a moralizing portrait a long way from her emotional confessions to Henrietta. Her love remained buried in the letters that she preserved like a hidden treasure, and in which twentieth-century biographers would find intact in all its wrenching power—to our greatest delight.[1]

Moffat, Edin.ᵗ Photo

Isabella L. Bird

A man whom any woman might love

Bird returned to Estes Park after her trip through the Rockies. That is when Jim Nugent declared his love for her. Bird described the scene that same evening in a letter to Henrietta:

"There is a tragedy about Mr. Nugent that has made me too terribly nervous. As soon as I had gone away he had discovered he was attached to me and it was killing him. It began on Long's Peak, he said. I was terrified, it made me shake all over and even cry. He is a man whom any woman might love but whom no sane woman would marry. Nor did he ask me to marry him. He knew enough for that. A less ungovernable nature would never have said a word, but his dark proud fierce soul all came out then."

Letter to Henrietta, November 18, 1873, quoted in Pat Barr, *A Curious Life for a Lady* (New York: Doubleday, 1970).

63

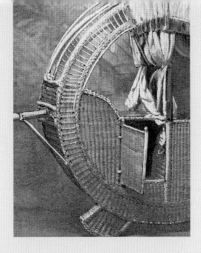

At last, an expedition
with an explicitly feminist twist:
May French-Sheldon was
a patent activist. So when
she left for Mount Kilimanjaro
in 1891, it was not to swoon
in ecstasy at the sight of the
vast Serengeti plain, nor to fulfill
a desperate need to go
one step further, nor even
to respond to the call of the
unknown. No, when she packed
her bags—and what bags!—it was
simply to prove that a woman
could be as good an explorer as
any man.

May French Sheldon

The White Queen

Her African expedition, meanwhile, was not the first challenge taken up by French-Sheldon, then aged forty-four. She had already been a scholar who specialized in French literature, a businesswoman, the founder and head of a prosperous publishing house, and the successful translator of Flaubert's *Salammbô*. In her spare time, she was the loving wife of a Mr. Sheldon who showed great indulgence toward his hyper active other half; and, last but not least, she was the only daughter of a couple of eccentric intellectuals, both from rich southern families (her father was a mathematics buff and her mother was keen on electrotherapy).

It seemed only natural that, after literature and business, May French-Sheldon should turn to travel. Exploration was fashionable in the West in the 1890s. Pith helmet, puttees, finger ready on the trigger yet equally ready with the pen: the caricatured picture of an explorer was already well anchored in the collective imagination. By that time, entire armies with cannon and collapsible boats were following the pioneering scouts who, twenty years earlier, had been solitary types in search of absolutes. The most famous of the slayers of the unknown was Henry Morton Stanley, who famously uttered, "Dr. Livingstone, I presume?", who helped to found the Congo Free State, and who, as it happened, was a friend of the Sheldon family. So it was hardly surprising that, as the nineteenth century drew to a close, May French-Sheldon set herself the goal of equaling the man she considered to be the paragon of civilizing courage.

In 1891, she made her decision: she would go exploring. It hardly mattered where, but she would head for Africa, because of Stanley, and more precisely for Kilimanjaro, because the name was so evocative. Setting herself such an aggressively feminist goal meant

THE COURT DRESS.

that failure was not an option. French-Sheldon planned her voyage like a military campaign. Organization was her strong point, fortunately, and her personal wealth enabled her to anticipate everything. Mrs. Sheldon vowed she would not suffer from hunger, heat, or cold.

Her husband was not allowed to come along, of course, for that would have invalidated the demonstration. Thus Mrs. Sheldon left alone, with the intention of recruiting women porters only; this would prove to be her sole setback, for in Zanzibar, where she completed her preparations, she managed to come up with only a single female porter. Thus she landed at Mombasa with three hundred men, whom she clothed in a manner that would protect her modesty.

It was predictable that this little band would question the competence of the strange woman who claimed she could lead them across Masai territory. Perhaps it was merely to test her that the porters mutinied on the first evening's march. Whatever the case, the explorer's response was swift:

Then or never I realized I must demonstrate to these mutinous, half-savage men that I would be obeyed, and that discipline should be enforced at any cost. Only for one instant in perplexity I paused, a vulture flew overhead, I drew my pistols and sent a bullet whizzing after it, and brought it surely down at my feet, to the astonishment of the revolting men.

With both pistols cocked, I suddenly became eloquent in the smattering of Swahali [sic] which I knew. . . .

"Every man who is not on his feet with his load on his head, when I have counted three, I will shoot!"

Street in *Mombasa*, B. E. *Africa.* 14. Juni. 05.

28 Anderson & Mayer, Proprietors, Mombasa.

That was the moment French-Sheldon became Bébé Bwana, the woman master or "White Queen." And, of course, the men obeyed, setting off on the march and following the White Queen right to the end.

French-Sheldon's goal was Lake Chala, some 6,500 feet high, at the foot of the snowy peak of Kilimanjaro, whose summit had already been scaled in 1889. The region was inhabited by the Rombo tribe, reputed to be hostile. Once French-Sheldon had mapped the lake and politely greeted the Rombos, she headed home, satisfied. She had made a contribution to science and had proven that the word "explorer" could apply to women. That was all.

The tale of French-Sheldon's adventures did not make readers shudder in horror, as had bestsellers published by Stanley, whose route had been encumbered with ferocious savages who had to be defeated with cannon. In fact, almost nothing befell the female explorer or her men, for one good reason as simple as it is laudable: not only did the feminist vow she would never suffer during her voyage, she also vowed that her porters would not suffer. Her marching day was calculated with respect to that principle; there was daily medical attention for every member of the troop, ranging from patching minor scratches to intensive care; the meals were monitored; and physical punishment was meted out to anyone who violated friendly behavior toward surrounding tribes. Indeed, French-Sheldon's sense of efficiency extended to everyone she came across; neither the Rombos nor even the fierce Masai warriors could undermine the White Queen's conviction that diplomatic methods

Pages 64 and 65: The palanquin in which May French-Sheldon traveled across one thousand miles of East Africa; portrait of May French-Sheldon.

Facing page: French-Sheldon in a "short" dress that offered a glimpse of her ankles; and resting in her palanquin.

Above: Postcard of a street in Mombasa, Kenya, northwest of Kilimanjaro.

Above: Despite various types of damage caused by the climate, a few negatives were successfully developed. This one shows a tribe's amazement on seeing French-Sheldon's camera.

Facing page: A caravan climbs to the heights of Kilimanjaro.

could always work, provided they were carried out with plenty of foresight and a good measure of spectacle.

Sheldon won her gamble—the expedition returned in more or less the same state as it set out, and not a single African felt aggrieved by her arrival. Indeed, the strange gifts brought by the White Queen—not to mention the amazing outfits she wore—were forever etched in her hosts' memories.

Unfortunately, twentieth-century readers preferred Stanley's bloody conquest over this apparently easy stroll by a feminist businesswoman. It was a stroll in appearance only, however, because French-Sheldon—determined to avoid the dreaded "I told you so"—played down an accident that occurred on the return journey. While the column of porters was crossing a swollen river, she was carried off by the current and dashed against a rock. Her spine was seriously injured, and the final part of her journey was torture, which she had to bear without wanting to display her pain. Her stoicism won her the admiration of her entourage, though at the price of indifference on the part of history. There is nevertheless no reason to feel sorry for French-Sheldon; once her victory had been accomplished and her book successfully published,[1] this upbeat woman recovered from her spinal injury just as she would, eventually, triumph over the oblivion into which she had fallen at the time of her death, aged eighty-nine, in 1936.

The White Queen's baggage

Garments included: a few jackets and short—that is, ankle-length—skirts, a white cotton suit with frogging, night dresses, a silk dress, three hats (one of felt, adorned with an ostrich feather, a second veiled with muslin, the third a wide-brimmed hat edged in gold); white gloves with gauntlets; an alpenstock marked with French-Sheldon's motto, *Noli me tangere* ("Do not touch me"); a ceremonial costume composed of a long gown of white silk embroidered with (imitation) jewels, a large baldric from which hung a medieval style sword (of tin); and a dagger (also tin, designed to be slid into her bodice), the whole topped by a long, blond wig.

Gifts and objects of barter included: beads, metal wire, silk, gold lace, British soldiers' coats (with plenty of brass buttons), red umbrellas, music boxes, pocket watches, kites, dolls, picture books, clay pipes, sewing machines, and several thousand rings engraved with her name.

Other items (not to mention ordinary objects) included: a spherical, wicker palanquin; a collapsible boat, a bathtub, a porcelain table service, silverware, folding tables and chairs, tablecloths, sheets, and medical supplies too lengthy to list. When walking, French-Sheldon wore a first-aid kit on her belt, containing essential pharmaceutical items ready for use.

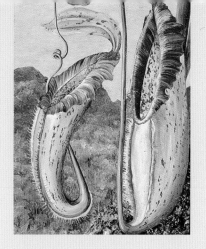

*M*arianne North's story is both unusual and unexceptional. Unusual because she was one of the greatest travelers in history, in terms of miles covered. Unexceptional because many Victorian ladies skipped across the continents, primly dressed and veiled, armed with a parasol, sometimes carrying an easel or a butterfly net, always equipped with a comfortable income and letters of introduction. They were all middle-aged spinsters, respectable yet solitary, obstreperous and yet genteel.

Marianne North

From Flower to Flower

North was forty when she faced up to the question: "What am I going to do now?" Her youthful years had been spent managing her father's house. Once he passed away, her horizons suddenly seemed simultaneously empty and overly cozy. She had sufficient funds, no need or desire to find a husband, and recalled that she had thoroughly enjoyed a trip she took with her father to the Holy Land. She thought about embarking on another voyage. But it was considered unworthy of an Englishwoman of 1871 to simply satisfy a whim: she was expected to do something to improve civilization or help humanity. North wasn't tempted by the idea of becoming a missionary. Nor a nurse—she had already spent the best years of her life caring for her father. But she didn't know how to do anything except paint flowers, a hobby she cultivated to occupy her spare time when nursing her father. Paint flowers? Well, why not?

Like many of her counterparts, North was organized, enterprising, and determined to conquer the world in her own way—by collecting all the flowers in it. She had her own special rules: never pick, always paint in oil, and always depict in a natural setting. Family friends encouraged her in this project, friends with names such as Charles Darwin, Francis Galton, and Joseph Hooker, all well-known scientists. Perhaps they were so enthusiastic because they thought it fashionable for spinsters to find an activity, and because they never imagined that she might find herself in danger when setting up her easel in front of the best British hotels around the globe.

They were certainly surprised to have been taken at their word so literally. Once she got started, North never stopped. Slowly, from year to year and from flower to flower, her endeavor evolved from

Pages 70 and 71: A plant painted by, and named after, Marianne North, *Nepenthes northiana*; a portrait of the naturalist at her easel.

Above: A panel painted by Marianne North showing a tea estate on Java in 1875.

Facing page: Two postcards of Ceylon.

scientific task to all-consuming passion—a passion for discovery and a passion for painting. In total, she clocked up two circumnavigations of the globe, each time making wide detours north and south. As her works accumulated, she commissioned and supervised the construction of what was immediately named the North Gallery, a building whose sole vocation was to house her paintings.

This globe-trotter never took excessive risks—she was not in quest of absolutes, and she wanted to hang on as long as possible to the nickname her nephews had given her, "Aunt Pop." She would settle in front of her subject—a flower—and become totally absorbed in her modest mission. It might be in Borneo, Ceylon, Jamaica, the Seychelles, Australia, Japan, Chile, the Cape of Good Hope, anywhere. She appreciated the surroundings and the scents, she would thank her hosts and sample exotic food, but she never wrestled with a crocodile or broached rapids in a dugout canoe. Photographs of her "in the field" inevitably show her sitting on a folding stool, leaning over a canvas, feet well shod, eyes shaded, fingers covered in paint.

Yet the results were not only fine, but monumental. Her trip to Brazil yielded over one hundred paintings; a voyage to India, two hundred. It is only fitting that her name is now recorded in botanical science, for five plants have been named in her honor, two of them her own discoveries: *Northia seychellana*, *Nepenthes northiana*, *Crinum northianum*, *Areca northiana*, and *Kniphofia northiae*.

Kandy Lake, Ceylon.

Tamil Lady in Rickshaw, Colombo, Ceylon.

It was only rheumatism and exhaustion that brought a halt to her travels. Sensibly—once again—she set down her trunks and her paintbrushes in order to die in her own bed in Gloucestershire, in 1890. But her flowers are immortal, as she had wished. The North Gallery remains one of the most popular attractions at the Royal Botanic Gardens at Kew, outside London, boasting 832 oil paintings that reflect a marked development toward a kind of highly personal Impressionism, a touching expression of travel fever combined with artistic exploration.

In the Seychelles, North paints an unknown tree, later classified as Northia seychellana

There were many of these trees on the island of Curieuse, and a path was cut to one of the biggest, with a pile of boulders behind it, on which I climbed, and perched myself on the top; my friends built a footstool for me from a lower rock just out of reach; I rested my painting-board on one of the great fan leaves, and drew the whole mass of fruit and buds in perfect security, though the slightest slip or cramp would have put an end both to the sketch and to me.

Marianne North, *Recollections of a Happy Life,* quoted in Dorothy Middleton, *Victorian Lady Travellers* (London: Routledge, 1965).

73

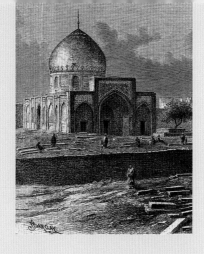

All lady travelers of the nineteenth century seemed highly attached to their femininity, though it is hard to know what to say about Jane Dieulafoy's femininity. Except that it was special. Indeed, Dieulafoy had a keen sense of dress, but her dress differed from that of her contemporaries: frock coat, vest, collar and tie, trousers and boots. The strange sight of Madame Dieulafoy, frail and blond yet resolutely masculine, was a curiosity of Parisian salons back in the 1880s. According to an eyewitness of the day she came across, theatrically speaking, as "a perfect male lead."

Jane Dieulafoy

Both Ways

Was it convenience or a sense of provocation that drove Dieulafoy to present herself on every occasion, from the most casual to the most official, the most Parisian to the most exotic, with her hair cut short and her curves hidden beneath a three-piece suit? We can be certain that when she donned male clothing for the first time in 1870, it was not pure whim. That was when Jane Dieulafoy, set off to join the man she had just married, military engineer Marcel Dieulafoy, at the battlefront against invading Prussian troops. Determined not to remain passive in the face of the threat to the nation, she wore a light-infantryman's uniform of gray trousers and tunic in order to take part in every mission.

This first experiment was a success. She would always remember how comfortable the outfit was, and when the Dieulafoys decided ten years later—Jane was then twenty-eight—to fulfill a joint dream by traveling to the Orient, Madame Dieulafoy left her dresses behind forever.

Their voyage of discovery of ancient Persia was considered an upper-class eccentricity by their entourage. Neither of them were archaeologists, and neither really knew what they were getting into. But they were enthusiastic about architecture, they formed a close couple, and they knew they could count on each other's courage, as already demonstrated during the war.

They would need their courage. In 1881, Persia was a land blighted by corruption and ravaged by looters. Their situation was all the more precarious since they were not on an official mission and they traveled without escort. The trails turned out to be patchy, the rivers flowed unpredictably, and the caravanserais were inhospitable hovels. The regional governors, meanwhile, were tyrannical potentates. Every trip was a leap into the unknown.

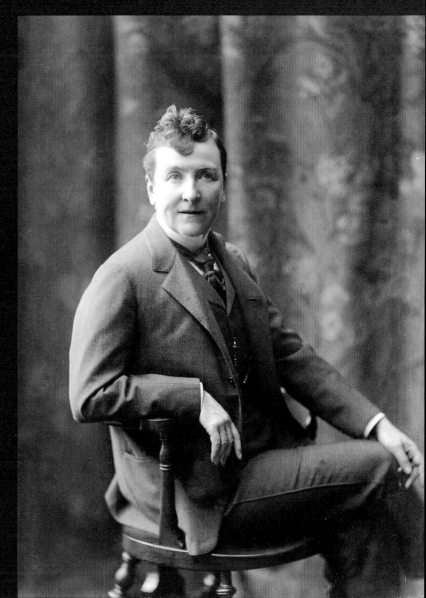

Madame Bienfaisy. — Dessin de E. Bayard, d'après une photographie.

In the fall of 1881 the couple arrived at the ruins of Susa, the ancient city of the Achaemenid dynasty, capital of Darius the Great. The site was a series of vague hillocks ravened by rains. Under the brambles, however, the Dieulafoys glimpsed columns and walls of mud brick. They left with a desire that would become an obsession: to excavate Susa and rescue Darius' palace from the oblivion into which it had fallen.

On their return to France, they organized an expedition—this time an official one backed by the director of French museums and the shah of Persia. In December 1884 they headed back to Susa. They would spend six months on the site in all, conducting two campaigns of excavation during which they uncovered the famous *Frieze of Archers* now on display in the Louvre. Thanks to this spectacular discovery, the European public would discover ancient Persia's incredible artistic wealth.

The day-to-day life of archaeologists back in 1885 was non-stop adventure. Violent rains would demolish excavation trenches, insects would invade the camp. "The flies arrive in such numerous legions that helmet and jacket seem to be covered in a jet-black shell; mosquitoes are armed with stingers so sharp they pierce clothing after having bored through the canvas of the campstool."[1] In that climate, meat rotted in two hours, milk went off even faster, getting supplies was difficult, and usually the only vegetables were the thistles and mauves that grew on the ruins. On the desert trail taken by the thirty mules and forty-three camels who carried the excavated treasures, the temperature ranged "between 59° and 67°C" (138°–150° F).

Pages 74 and 75: Tomb and cemetery at Shushtar, Iran (drawing by Barclay, based on an expedition photograph); Jane Dieulafoy in the privacy of her Parisian salon on rue Chardin, Passy, c. 1900.

Facing page, clockwise: Transporting archaeological equipment (drawing by Ferdinandus, based on an expedition photograph); Jane Dieulafoy, aged thirty, in the clothing she wore when traveling through Persia in 1881–1882; Jane and Marcel Dieulafoy, Babin, and Houssay sheltering from torrential rain under an Arab tent during their first expedition to Susa in 1884 (drawing by Myrbach).

Above: Jane confronts marauders on the banks of the Kerkha River, outside Susa. "I have fourteen bullets at my disposal! Go get six of your friends!" (Drawing by Tofani, based on a sketch by Marcel Dieulafoy, 1888.)

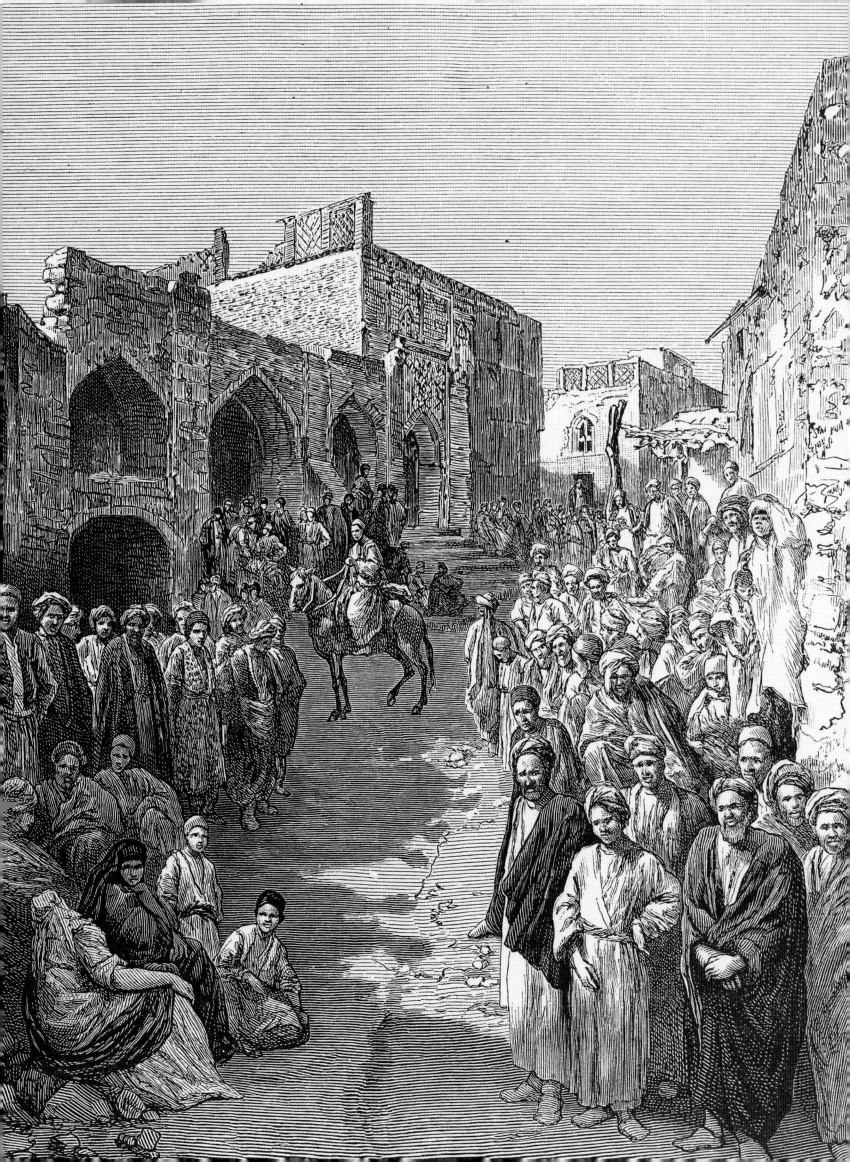

Whatever difficulties they endured, by the time the amateur archaeologists returned to Paris everyone was convinced of one thing: Madame Dieulafoy didn't merely follow her husband, she marched alongside him, determined to be a full part of the adventure and, similarly, to fully enjoy its fruits. It was Jane, moreover, who wrote the articles that would be serialized in *Le Tour du Monde*. Famous and admired, Jane was more than just a curiosity, she was an exception. No other woman in France of the 1890s had earned the right to be herself to such an extent, free to choose what she wanted to wear, what job she wanted to do, and what status she sought, without being considered a fallen woman. It was her affectionate partnership with her husband that allowed her to occupy this unique place in women's history.

For that matter, Jane Dieulafoy never sought to turn her hard-earned liberty into a feminist campaign. She thought only of the Orient. All her articles betray the passion she felt for the region. From Constantinople eastward she was carried away by a sense of wonder; never, despite malaria and dysentery, despite death threats from local chieftains and plagues of parasites (she was forced to shave her head to rid herself of lice), did she waver in her feelings. Ten years later, when she had become a literary figure, an original and well-known member of intellectual circles, she would still say that she had left part of her heart in Persia. She also left her health there; drained by amebic dysentery that had hounded her for years, she died on May 25, 1916, in the arms of her husband, following one last archaeological trip to Morocco.

Facing page: Main street, Shushtar, in 1886 (engraving by Bertrand, drawing by Marcelle Lancelot, based on a photograph by Jane Dieulafoy).

Above: Jane Dieulafoy in the Hor on a January night (drawing by Tofani, based on a sketch by Marcel Dieulafoy).

Above: Lori workers bustling around an excavation (drawing by Taylor, based on an expedition photograph).

Right: frieze showing a lion, discovered by the Dieulafoys (drawing by Marcel Dieulafoy).

Below right: the house that served as expedition headquarters in Bushir, Iran (drawing by Barclay, based on an expedition photograph).

Facing page: The Guard of Immortals, based on a drawing by Barclay.

Four bullets shattered the stone

When being presented to Sheikh Ali, a nomadic chieftain near the Susa ruins, Jane Dieulafoy (called Khanum, "Lady") was hailed by one of the sheikh's relatives, who was organizing a shooting contest with his French visitors:

"'The Khanum has to fire, too,' cried one of the Arabs. Khanum hesitated—was she going to jeopardize the reputation of her comrades, or admit that women in Farangustan [France] were made of different stuff than men? They insisted. I set one knee on the ground, shouldered the rifle: four times my bullets shattered the stone and raised a triumphant cloud of dust. Shouts of enthusiasm concluded this little salvo. The Arabs ran up to touch my weapon and the hem of my garments. 'May God bless you and keep you!,' etc. 'We're safe from attack for a while!'"

Jane Dieulafoy, *En mission chez les Immortels: Journal des fouilles du Suse,* 1884–86 (Paris: Éditions Phébus, 1990).

81

*F*anny Vandegrift liked lively, whimsical, impatient men; men for whom the main thing was to keep moving, as Robert Louis Stevenson liked to say. She followed her first man into the Nevada desert, and would follow the second to a Pacific isle. Yet even though her two husbands had cheerful temperaments, they gave Fanny as much grief as pleasure. Barely had Sam Osbourne married the sixteen-year-old Fanny than he left Indiana, where the Vandegrifts lived, to fight in the Civil War.

Fanny Stevenson

"Indifference impossible"

Once the war was over, he left again, this time to become a prospector in Nevada, all the way across the continent. He was drawn not so much by the idea of striking it rich as a desire to be part of the opening of the Far West. When he asked Fanny to join him there, she didn't hesitate. With their little five-year-old daughter in one hand, she took a train from Indiana to New York, then a boat for Panama, then crossed the isthmus, sailed up to San Francisco, then found a coach going to Austin, Nevada. The voyage lasted forty-seven days and required crossing forty miles of Panamanian swampland, partly on foot.

The terminus was Virginia City, a small mining town that had sprung from the desert. Although Sam had found neither gold nor silver, he had acquired many friends—and a mistress. Fanny was not about to return to the family fold, however. Having become a pioneer, she experienced the life of gold prospectors: log cabins, rattlesnakes, fear of thirst, fear of Indians. Sam may well have thought he'd married a totally devoted woman, but he was wrong. If Fanny stayed, it was not from marital duty but because she wanted to prove herself, and she wanted to put up a fight.

In 1868, after the birth of a second child, she finally wearied of a husband who no longer seemed so funny. So Mrs. Osbourne headed back east: first on the ship, then across the isthmus, another ship, the train—only to retrace her steps almost immediately, in the hope that it was still possible to save her marriage. From 1869 to 1875, the Osbournes presented the image of a normal family, but Fanny was increasingly uneasy with the role of obedient little wife. In an effort to carve out a life for herself, she took up painting. She enjoyed it so much that she began to dream of becoming an artist.

Now, in those days the greatest artists all lived in Europe. So she dreamed of leaving—and she left. After having wrangled Sam's consent, she sailed for Antwerp with their three children, the youngest of whom, Hervey, was only five. By the fall of 1875 she was in Paris, where she began taking courses in painting. She wrote that she found the French way of painting very appealing, but that she still didn't know very much about it. Unfortunately, she didn't get a chance to broaden her knowledge. Hervey fell ill and Fanny's life became consumed by treatments, medicines, bedside care, and finally the unbearable sight of the child's death throes—Sam joined his wife in the spring of 1876, just in time to see Hervey die in dreadful agony. The memory of it would haunt Fanny all her life.

Sam went back to America. But not Fanny. She spent the summer with her two surviving children, Belle and Lloyd, in an inn on the edge of the forest of Fontainebleau, where all the bohemian artists of Paris and London liked to gather in order to paint.

That was where a young Scottish writer first set eyes on the American woman in mourning. He noticed her forthright gaze, the cigarette in her hand, the image of liberty and maternity—and he fell in love. Robert Louis Stevenson was nine years younger than Fanny, but the "foreign goddess," as he called her, was made for him. His certainty never waved on that point. Like Sam, Louis laughed easily, was liked by children, and was constantly on the move. He differed, though, in being constantly unwell. His appetite for travel was also

an endless quest for sun, fresh air, mountains—anything that could ease his tubercular cough.

Fanny had no objections to the role of nurse and mother that the young Scottish writer was implicitly asking her to play. But the role of mistress—of fallen woman—frightened her. She fled back to California, to Sam, in the hope of saving their marriage once again. But barely had the two new lovers been separated than they realized just how entwined their lives already were, for better or for worse. To a telegram that Fanny sent him July 1879, Louis replied that he would drop everything and join her within the month. So he left Scotland for California. He arrived on schedule, out of strength, and had to bide his time in Monterey while Fanny negotiated a divorce that would leave her custody of the children. Barely had Fanny and Louis married, on May 19, 1880, than the quest for sun and fresh air recommenced, frantically, from mountain to mountain and beach to beach, interspersed with the publication of several masterpieces such as *Treasure Island* (which Louis invented for—and with—Fanny's son, Lloyd), *The Silverado Squatters, The Master of Ballantrae, Dr. Jekyll and Mr. Hyde,* and *In the South Seas.* Fanny and Louis had arrived in those South Seas in 1890, where it seemed they finally found a haven. After wandering from island to island, they reached Samoa, at last finding the pleasant life they had almost given up seeking, having tried Switzerland, the English coast, the French Riviera, New York State, Hawaii, and Australia. They finally settled down, buying a property on the isle of Apia. More major books followed, such as

Pages 82 and 83: Robert Louis Stevenson, detail from an oil painting by John Singer Sargent, 1885; and a portrait of Fanny Osbourne around the time she met Stevenson.

Facing page: Robert Louis Stevenson on the schooner *Equator*; and a portrait of Fanny in 1883.

Above: On an island in the South Seas, Fanny and Robert Louis Stevenson welcoming a British navy band and Samoans at Vailima.

Strong *paust* | mary | m.J.S | Lloyd | R.L.S. | Fanny | Simi. Butler
Savea | Elena | Talojo cook | austin. Belle | Lapaolo | Tomasi
Plantation boy | Laundress | arrick | | Cattleman | assistant Cook
| | Pantry man |
| | Black boy. Simelel. |

Above, clockwise: The Stevenson family with their servants and Samoans on the porch of their house at Vailima; Fanny and Robert Louis Stevenson in the company of Nantiki and Natakauti on Butaritari, an atoll in Kiribati; Fanny's funeral ceremony, celebrated on the summit of Mount Vaea on June 23, 1915, twenty-one years after her husband's death.

Facing page: The last photograph of Robert Louis Stevenson, taken in 1893.

Catriona and *Our Samoan Adventure* (written with Fanny). Louis wasn't able to enjoy his new-found paradise for long, however: he died in 1894 of apoplexy, aged forty-four. In accordance with his wishes, Fanny had him buried at the top of Mount Vaea. For nearly ten years she tried to keep up the estate founded by Louis, but finally gave up and sailed back to San Francisco.

Her life was not over, however. She still loved joyous men. And joyous men still loved her back. "She was pretty as a young woman," wrote her sister Nellie, "but as she grew older she was beautiful." The men were Gelett Burgess, followed by Ned Field. They were her secretaries by profession, her lovers by choice, despite some thirty years' difference in age. "She was the only woman in the world worth dying for," wrote Ned Field.[1] On she went, to London, Paris, and the Riviera, until the age of seventy-three; she continued to flitter around until February 17, 1914, when she died peacefully in her sleep. Her final voyage was to Samoa, to the summit of Mount Vaea, where her ashes now rest beside Robert Louis Stevenson.

Fanny Stevenson, the Weird Woman
Native name: Tamaitai

If you don't get on with her, it's a pity about your visit. She runs the show . . . . A violent friend, a brimstone enemy . . . . Is always either loathed or slavishly adored; indifference impossible. The natives think her uncanny and that devils serve her. Dreams dreams, and sees visions.

Letter from Robert Louis Stevenson to James Barrie, April 2, 1893.
Selected Letters of Robert Louis Stevenson, edited by Ernest Mehew (New Haven: Yale University Press, 2001), p. 536.

It was a close call—Mary Kingsley might never have been able to become the great ethnographic traveler she eventually became. It took a wedding ceremony, just four days prior to her birth. Her father, in fact, long hesitated before giving his name to the servant who bore his child; if he hadn't done so, Mary Kingsley would have been an illegitimate child raised in shame and poverty by an uneducated mother.

Mary Kingsley

The Hippopotamus and the Umbrella

Fortunately, George Kingsley, a doctor and a traveler himself, decided at the last minute "to do the right thing." Mary was therefore given the education of a well-to-do young lady and she profited from the scholarship typical of the entire Kingsley family.

That did not make her childhood happy, however. George abandoned home soon after his daughter's birth and recommenced his globe trotting life, while his wife sank into melancholy and progressively turned her daughter into a nurse. The young woman's seclusion nevertheless contained one treasure. "I had a great amusing world of my own [that] other people did not know or care about—the books in my father's library."

Boredom and solitude were thus the source of Mary's future. She read Burton, Livingstone, Brazza, du Chaillu, and others. She acquired a consuming interest in Africa, even though she had never explored any further than the streets close to home, first in London and later in Cambridge. Her fascination grew during the fifteen years she spent at her mother's bedside, outwardly docile and self-effacing. But ultimately she was delivered from bondage when her parents died, one after the other; in those days, death was the only way the self-sacrificing spinsters could acquire their freedom.

She set sail one year later, in 1893, aged thirty. With her black dress and her hair drawn tightly to the back of her head, Miss Kingsley appeared to be the perfect champion of Victorian England. This time, however, appearances were misleading. Everything that normally shocked her fellow females delighted Kingsley—African customs, "wildness," and even the shady world of adventurers who dominated trade along the Congo. Although she had headed to West Africa "to die," as she willingly admitted, she found that Africa

Pages 88 and 89: Mary Kingsley was highly intrigued by the Fang people of Gabon, who were thought to be cannibals (*Travels in West Africa*, 1893–95); a portrait of Kingsley, aged thirty-four.

Above, and right: The Fang, armed with guns, were known to be the main suppliers of ivory. Fang people dressed for the ceremonial voodoo dance of death.

Facing page: A makeshift hospital in Major Ford's camp in Paordelerg, South Africa, during the Boer War, January 1, 1900.

"amused me and was kind to me and scientifically interesting and did not want to kill me just then."

Kingsley wasn't content merely to play the Romantic traveler, however. She wanted to be useful. Thus she collected specimens of fish for the British Museum, and collected fetishes for herself. She also built up a collection of anecdotes that, strung together in her books, lent an inimitable quality to her tales:

> Once a hippopotamus and I were on an island together, and I wanted one of us to leave. I preferred it should be myself, but the hippo was close to my canoe, and looked like staying, so I made cautious and timorous advances to him and finally scratched him behind the ear with my umbrella and we parted on good terms. But with the crocodile it was different.[1]

She returned to London in 1884, but set off again almost immediately. When her younger brother asked, in all innocence, that she

care for him the way she had cared for her mother, she flatly refused
and decided to flee. After the Congo she visited Sierra Leone and
Gabon, sailed up the Ogowé River, first on a steamer and then in a
dugout canoe. There she stayed among the Fang, then made an
ascent of Mount Cameroon. Everywhere she introduced herself as a
trader, just a merchant like any another. She swapped bolts of cloth
for rubber and ivory, which financed her travels even as it made it
easier for Africans to accept her. A decidedly unpredictable character,
she seemed at ease in the ungenteel circles that she defended in her
writings: "I have no hesitation in saying that in the whole of West
Africa, in one week, there is not one-quarter of the drunkenness you
can see any Saturday night you choose in a couple of hours in the
Vauxhall Road."

She was being unpredictable once again when she
denounced what Kipling's fans liked to call "the white man's
burden." In her second book, she openly criticized colonial
authorities and missionaries for ignoring an ethnological
approach to African peoples in favor of a policy based on "good
intentions, ignorance, and Maxim guns." Such comments earned
her a Colonial Office description as "the most dangerous woman
on the other side."

Without ever dropping her schoolteacherly manner, Kingsley
had ways of liberating herself. So even though she could proclaim
that, "as for encasing the more earthward extremities of my anatomy
in trousers, I would rather perish on the public scaffold," she could
also transform her London apartment into an exotic hothouse

Above: British soldiers relaxing in South Africa, January 1, 1900.

Facing page: Mary Kingsley in mourning dress for her parents, 1892.

bedecked with African masks, and could stroll down the streets of London with a monkey on her shoulder.

Her humor being as unyielding as her morals, Kingsley became wildly popular in fin-de-siècle London. Her books sold well, and her lectures were packed. Her final voyage nevertheless demonstrated that she ultimately remained a patriotic Englishwoman rather than "the most dangerous woman" in the anticolonial movement. For this time she sailed for the Cape as a volunteer nurse in prisoner camps in South Africa, then in the grip of the Boer War. She died there, in Simonstown, on June 3, 1900, of typhoid fever caught from her patients.

The finest tribute to her was the founding of the Royal African Society, whose goal was to make known "the laws and customs of the Africans" in the goal of better understanding between the white and black worlds. The first meeting was convened, symbolically, in Kingsley's Kensington parlor on June 26, 1900.

1862 – 1900.

Mary Kingsley.

Scott & Wilkinson

CAMBRIDGE.

The reckless abandon of a Sarah Bernhardt

Once when Kingsley's canoe was in danger of overturning in the rapids of the Ogowé, the head boatman ordered the white woman to scramble across the rocks to the shore.

"The inhabitants of the village, seeing we were becoming amusing again, came, legging it like lamp-lighters, after us, young and old, male and female, to say nothing of the dogs. Some good souls helped the men haul, while I did my best to amuse the others by diving headlong from a large rock to which I had elaborately climbed, into a thick clump of willow-leaved shrubs. They applauded my performance vociferously, and then assisted my efforts to extricate myself, and during the rest of my scramble they kept close to me, with keen competition for the front row, in hopes that I would do something like it again. But I refused the *encore*, because, bashful as I am, I could not but feel that my last performance was carried out with all the superb reckless *abandon* of a Sarah Bernhardt, and a display of art of this order should satisfy any African village for a year at least."

Mary Kingsley, *Travels in West Africa* [1897] (Mineola, NY: Dover, 2003).

In 1898, Fanny Bullock Workman launched her assault on the Himalayas. Hanging from the handlebars of her bicycle was a tin teakettle. Her pith helmet harbored the badge of the Touring Club de France. A final accessory, one that never left her side and was scarcely less indispensable than her teakettle, was her husband.

It had been nearly ten years since the two Americans—she now aged thirty-nine, he forty-two—had set off to cycle around the world. Since 1889, to be exact, the year they crossed the Atlantic for a cultural tour after poor health obliged Dr. Workman to go into early retirement. Cycling must have been just what the doctor ordered for this sickly physician, because the couple successively visited France, Italy, Spain, Algeria, and Morocco, steadily adding to their cycling equipment such items as a whip (to drive away the dogs who chased Mrs. Workman's skirts), a pistol (for any men similarly inclined), and a Kodak camera.

In 1898, the couple landed at Cape Comorin after having visited Ceylon. Their goal was to travel up the length of India right to the Himalayas, the "Roof of the World." This itinerary meant cycling one thousand five hundred miles—the longest single leg would be eighty-five miles—on trails sometimes sandy, sometimes muddy, in temperatures over 100° F. We do not know how Dr. Workman's allegedly poor health stood up to it.

By summer, the couple reached the foot of the mountains. They abandoned bicycles for alpenstocks, and set off on their first trek, from Srinagar to Ladakh via the Karakoram pass. It was a revelation. After one more cycle tour—of Java—they were convinced that a chapter was coming to a close. Having traveled all those miles, they decided that the human spectacle was rather disappointing compared to nature's dramatic show. Henceforth, the Himalayas would be their realm of conquest.

The Roof of the World, as it is sometimes known, was still poorly mapped and eminently hostile at that time. It called for boldness and endurance. The Workmans would henceforth spend all

their time in the Himalayas, except when reporting on their latest discoveries to the Royal Geographical Society. Delivering these reports was itself a new barrier to be overcome, for even at the dawn of the twentieth century Britain's gentlemen geographers hesitated to open their doors to ladies. But this particular lady had no intention of letting her husband speak on her behalf, even when it involved challenging the discoveries of their predecessors or correcting poorly calculated altitudes—in short, attacking the scientific community. In a sign that the times were changing, however, the Society listened to her. In fact, the Workmans' expeditions represented a bridge between the new century and the old: they embodied the twentieth-century spirit of organization, logistical support, use of professional guides, careful photography of all exploits, and sense of publicity, yet they retained nineteenth-century attitudes when it came to sherpas—"coolies" in their parlance—who were viewed as beasts of burden rather than admirable mountaineers, to the lofty lyricism of their descriptions of nature, and, above all, to the indescribable blanket-like dresses that Fanny insisted on wearing whatever the altitude, snow conditions, or distance to be covered in a day.

The list of their achievements makes the head spin. It is hard to imagine how Fanny and William found the time to have a child—a little girl named Rachel—in the course of their frenzied career:

1899: three summits conquered and duly measured during a single voyage.

1902–03: exploration of a glacier some twenty-five miles long (Chogo Lungma, in the Karakorams). This expedition enabled them to correct maps of the region, which they felt were inaccurate, although it would in fact turn out that the Workmans, not their predecessors, were mistaken—from which it emerged that they had not climbed the right summit (itself an amusing accomplishment, since the ascension was an exploit nonetheless).

1906: exploration of Nun Kun range, after which they once again wrongly claimed to have scaled its highest peak (the highest, Nun, would indeed be climbed for the first time by a woman, but not until 1953, by Frenchwoman Claude Kogan).

They nevertheless continued to add to their list of "firsts":

1908: the Hispar glacier;

1911 and 1912: Siachen, a glacier over forty miles long. This expedition would be their last, and also the one that specialists agree was truly exceptional. Yet this time Fanny herself, contemplating the raging snowmelt rivers she would have to cross, admitted that she was on the point of giving up. "'No, I won't come again,' I said as I

Pages 94 and 95: The eastern slope of Hispar glacier; a portrait of Fanny Bullock Workman in September 1910.

Facing page, clockwise: Fanny in front of the Jagannath Temple in Puri; on the Chamundi hills of Mysore, India; and in the privacy of her mountaineering tent at the foot of the Shafat glacier.

Above: Fanny and William Workman cross the Zak River in India, accompanied by sherpas (*Ice-Bound Heights of the Mustagh*, 1908).

Above, clockwise: Bare-footed sherpas scale the Sher-pi-gang glacier in the Karakoram range; the Workmans on the Jhula bridge spanning the Indus (*Ice-Bound Heights of the Mustagh*, 1908); Fanny crosses a river on Rose glacier on a sherpa's back (*Two Summers in the Ice Wilds of the Eastern Karakoram*, 1917)

Facing page: Fanny is caught in a crevasse (*In the Ice World of the Himalaya*, 1900).

sat snowed up in my tent for two days... in September 1911. But no sooner had I turned by back to the [glacier] ... than my mountain-ego asserted itself, saying '*tant pis*' to the obstacles, 'Return you must.'"

This final, brilliant expedition also provided the opportunity to stage a memorable image: a woman in the snow holding a sign clearly reading, "Votes for Women." To judge by the hat and dress, it might look as though the photo was taken during an outing on the Mer de Glace just above Chamonix, France. But Fanny was actually in one of the most dangerous mountain ranges in the world, and she had to hold her sign with both hands to prevent high-altitude winds from whipping it away. This picture makes it easy to forgive her for having been an occasionally presumptuous mountaineer.

Fanny Bullock Workman, suffragette and pioneer of extreme mountaineering, died in 1925. She left behind a bereft but indestructible husband, who lived for another thirteen years, to the age of eighty.

Space in a crevasse

Here we roped as it was necessary to move with caution. The lightly-loaded coolies followed in our *spoor*. It is needless to say, that, with the wet snow and water under it, our pedal extremities did not suffer from dryness.

The fatigue occasioned by a march can seldom be estimated by the number of hours required to accomplish it, and, certainly that afternoon on Snow Lake may be counted as one of the most fatiguing afternoons on the Biafo. With all due care, we were constantly in snow or crevasses, to above the knees, and one of the party will not soon forget the sensation she felt on disappearing up to her shoulders in one of the latter.

Zubriggen said, "Pull on the rope and push back with the feet." This is good advice, when there is anything to push against, but pushing against space in a crevasse accomplishes little, and pulling on a rope, when one's arm are embedded in snow, is about equally futile, but finally, by strenuous efforts on her part and hauling on that of the guide, she came out again. This form of exercise continued until half-past four, when we began the ascent of an ice slant, where each step had to be cut. This took some time, at a height of over 16,000 feet.

Quoted in Dorothy Middleton, *Victorian Lady Travellers* (London: Routledge, 1965).

1890–1918

Between Two Worlds

Why They Wrote

"To travel is to write."
Against all expectation, the trailblazing women of the transitional era shared Marcel Proust's highly contemplative outlook on life. Like him, they were convinced that "real life, a life finally revealed and illumined, hence the only life truly lived, is—a work of literature!"

Some of these women felt sympathy for humanity, while others had a love of nature, yet all experienced a passion to which they were devoted—a passion for books. Before becoming women of action, the likes of Gertrude Bell, Isabelle Eberhardt, and Alexandra David-Néel were great readers.

"Writing is like loving"

Isabelle Eberhardt

Before setting off in quest of their own truths, vanquishing their patient suffering and isolation, learning to keep in touch with their feelings—as required by their future victories and their survival in the field—the great travelers first sought themselves in literature. As girls and young women, they took refuge in poetry or adventure novels. They fled in reverie, rescued from the feeling of being different, alone, and frustrated by the inventions and accounts of others. Their long-felt desire to escape initially took root in the imagination.

Alexandra David-Néel admitted that she had long "dreamed of becoming a Jules Verne hero," and that as a child she had plunged into *Around the World in Eighty Days, The Black Indies,* and *Tribulations of a Chinaman in China.* Then, as a haughty and rebellious teenager, she devoured Epictetus and Marcus Aurelius, and practiced living a tough life, oblivious to suffering, just like those Stoic philosophers.

Such inspiration might be philosophical, novelistic, or purely literary.

It was Isabelle Eberhardt's consumption of novels such as Pierre Loti's *Roman d'un Spahi* and *Aziyadé* that set her on the road toward the Orient. Yet she almost certainly chose North Africa as her specific destination due to the lyrical letters—full of poetic descriptions of the desert—that she received from her brother, who had enlisted in the French Foreign Legion.

"Oxford!" exclaimed Gertrude Bell, "Oxford!" she repeated at her delight on finding herself wandering among the shelves of the Bodleian Library, the most amazing of all university libraries. "Can you believe it?" she asked her parents. "Here I can borrow hundreds of books!" Upon discovering the Bodleian Library, the *Thousand and One Nights,* and the beauty of Oriental languages, Bell began heading down the path that would lead to the major adventure of her life: Baghdad.

A taste for literature leads to travel. And sometimes literature even makes departure possible—Eberhardt financed the start of her nomadic life by becoming a writer. Even before she moved to the Orient, she wrote short stories and attempted to conquer the world of letters (another adventurer, Lydie Paschkoff, who lived by her pen in Paris and published her own travel books, advised and steered Eberhardt). David-Néel, meanwhile, took up cutting-edge journalism, writing to refute common misconceptions—her first, hundred-page essay was so contentious that Paris publishers wouldn't touch it, and David-Néel had to have it published in Brussels. Yet only ten years later, Parisian publishing houses would be clamoring for her books—her *Voyage d'une Parisienne à Lhassa* made the fortune of Les Éditions Plon.

Ella Maillart, meanwhile, stated it clearly: she went after publishing contracts in order to pay for her voyages. "I write only to travel." Such humbleness from such a great writer. Maillart, Eberhardt, and David-Néel—not to overlook Karen Blixen, when it comes to writing talent—were born women of letters. "For me, writing is like loving, because that is probably my fate. And my sole consolation," admitted Eberhardt, so closely linked to her literary projects that she confused them with her life's plans.

A few trailblazers—including some of the greatest—produced literary masterpieces. But what of the others, the four hundred female travelers who wrote and published accounts of their expeditions? "It is necessary to write," commented Vita Sackville-West in

"It is necessary to write if the days are not to slip emptily by"

Vita Sackville-West

her *Account of a Journey Across the Bakhtiari Mountains,* "if the days are not to slip emptily by . . . for the moment passes, it is forgotten; the mood is gone; life itself is gone!" For all these women, the desire to communicate was at the heart of their solitary exploits. For all of them, adventure and literature were an integral part of their process of survival, and would remain firmly linked.

Passing on acquired knowledge implies the return of the traveler. The self *has* to survive in order to bear witness to what has been experienced. Thus an absolute determination to leave an account of things can help to overcome serious difficulties. And the need to stay alive is contained in the very idea of a tale—recounting the adventure is a way of holding on to it. And publishing a tale means continuing it, making it last, and ultimately immortalizing it, insuring the survival of countless discoveries made during the voyage.

Yet it is hard to convey the discipline, courage, and effort required to scribble in a notebook every night. Hard to appreciate the exhaustion of staying up at night after a harrowing day while all around you the guides, interpreters, and porters are sleeping. Alone, by the light of a candle, pen in hand, among the mosquitoes and centipedes, these women still had to make their way through the jungle of language, stumbling over words, getting bogged down in phrases, struggling to get the day's tribulations down in writing.

Tibetans in the sacred city of Lhasa, which had not yet been sullied by the presence of a Western white woman, didn't give a second thought to the contents of the bundles carried by a decrepit beggarwoman. And why should they? How could they imagine its contents? Nothing set David-Néel apart from the other poor women, nothing could give her away—not her rags, worn bonnet,

ink-dyed hair, yak-hair pigtails, and ash-darkened complexion—nothing could give her away except the stacks of paper she was carrying in her bag. Pages and pages of writing in English, French, and Tibetan.

What wellsprings of energy she must have deployed in order to write all those volumes in secret! Forgetting nothing, leaving nothing out. Saying it all. Despite the fear, the fatigue, the cold: write, write, and write some more. To nurture the seeds of all the books that would recount her mountain journeys, her encounters with people, her discovery of Lamaism—over twenty books that would reveal the mystery and grandeur of Tibet to the world. Twenty books, plus the hundreds of letters she wrote to her husband.

If women adventurers sought the world's hidden meaning, beyond all borders and appearances, they also attempted to go ever higher, ever further, thanks to words. André Malraux followed them in this vein when he compared travelers to creative writers who extend the frontiers of language to its limits. So maybe female trailblazers are part of the race of poets, perhaps their own lives should be seen as poems in motion.

"Once you've been up there," claimed David-Néel, "there's absolutely nothing left to see or do. Life—a life such as mine, which was just one long desire to travel—is over, has attained its final goal. . . . Blessed," she continued, "blessed are those who achieve their dream. That, too, is a blessing, and not the least!"

A. L.

"They could marvel at people as well as landscapes"

Christel Mouchard

With the Tip of a Parasol

More confident than her predecessors, the Traveler no longer sought to prove that she was "a proper lady." It had already been demonstrated that a woman could travel and remain a virgin, could love both geography and embroidery. In 1900, the trunks of women explorers still contained silks, lace, corsets. And although the wardrobe might be padded with a jellaba or Asian tunic, those items always carried an indescribable air of fashion and femininity—though of the generous, rather than virtuous, kind.

Women travelers were more relaxed, less conquering. They no longer brandished civilization and religion before them—they could henceforth marvel at people as well as landscapes. They even dared to fight for their ideas, to plant the suffragette flag on Himalayan peaks, to take up the cause of Aboriginal peoples before a wholly male audience, to defend—with the tip of a parasol, or the tip of a pen—oppressed men and women, human differences. Even though almost all of these women remained little islands of Westernness that drifted from one continent to another, even though many continued to view themselves as ambassadors of their native countries, their view of the world was slowly changing. As they traveled among foreign populations they could henceforth make friends, encounter equals, and—on occasion—even consider marriage.

As Lawrence of Arabia used to say, she should be called Bell of Baghdad. Gertrude Bell's adventure among the Bedouin chiefs of Mesopotamia was, in fact, a female pendant to Colonel Lawrence's efforts in Arabia.

The pair had striking points in common: both were fascinated by the lords of the desert, both threw themselves headlong into the free, tough life of the nomads, both were scholarly archaeologists even as they served as secret agents for the British Crown, and both were consulted as advisors by the international conferences that led to the Treaty of Sèvres.

Gertrude Bell

Bell of Baghdad

Finally, both came to a tragic end—Lawrence died in a motorcycle accident on a country road, Bell committed suicide in Baghdad at the height of her fame, in 1926.

Fame had been promised to her at birth, in 1868. That, at least, was her personal conviction, seconded by her first and greatest admirer—her father.

Wonderfully elegant, witty, bold, and bright, Bell decided at any early age that her life would differ from others. Her family encouraged this conceit, fortunately compensated by a solid sense of humor. Accepted at Oxford, she graduated with a first-class degree in modern history. But that was not enough for Bell; when nearly thirty, after a brief, thwarted engagement, she decided to climb the Alps. "What do you think?" she wrote to her father, saying she had climbed "seven new peaks, one of them first class and four very good."

Then she headed for the deserts, staying in Jerusalem, Damascus, and Baghdad as the invitations arrived from diplomatic friends of the family. She began taking "excursions" that went further and further abroad. Soon she was speaking fluent Arabic, and wouldn't hesitate to spend all day on horseback or camel, ignoring the travel restrictions imposed by the Ottoman authorities (the entire Middle East was still under Turkish domination at that time). In March 1900, she ventured into the land of Moab with mules, a guide, and an escort imposed by the Ottomans. Shortly after her return, she managed to head into Druze country by giving her escort the slip.

Her first real expedition took place in 1905, in the Syrian desert. Meeting Bedouin tribesmen who had never seen a Western

woman became something of a sport for Bell, which annoyed the Turkish occupiers but delighted her British compatriots. Indeed, Miss Bell was sufficiently intelligent and cultivated to make observations during her travels that the Crown would find very useful in due course, even as she was making unexpected acquaintance with her nomadic hosts. "I gave him my visiting card," she said of Sheikh Ibn Farhan, "and he bade me welcome to all the Shammar tents." The method might seem surprising, but it worked, particularly since Gertrude Bell's air of aristocratic ease inevitably appealed to the lords of the desert.

Even when concentrating on archaeology, in which she had a solid background, Bell continued to establish connections, take notes, make observations. She gathered information and contacts the way other voyagers collected flowers or butterflies, building up a living collection of friendships that she cultivated month after month thanks to mutual esteem, erudition, and savoir-faire. Yet there was nothing ethnographic in her approach, and she never hid her own convictions: although she admired the Arab feudal system, she was working above all for the grandeur of the British Empire, and secondly for science. She never fought for feminism, a struggle she despised, judging it injurious to superior women like herself, who didn't need the right to vote to reveal all their abilities.

In May 1907, aged thirty-nine, she was in Asia Minor studying Armenian churches when she met Charles Doughty-Wylie. "There is an English v. consul here now, a charming young soldier with quite a pleasant little wife. He is the more interesting of the two, a good type

of Englishman, wide awake and on the spot, keen to see and learn." Without realizing it, the traveler was falling in love. Doughty-Wylie, meanwhile, remained faithful to his wife but was wildly attracted to this most unusual woman. A strange love affair sprang up. In order to respect the moral values they both shared, they made a surprising decision, one that would certainly be harder for her than for him. "I shall never be your lover, my dear," Charles wrote to Gertrude, "never your lover, that is, man to woman. But what we can have, we will keep and cherish. Yes, we will be wise and gentle, as you said." During the whole duration of their affair, Charles and Gertrude met no more than ten times. But their steady correspondence betrays a sensuality that matched their frustration. "And so closes our little time alone," wrote Charles after a brief reunion. "We shall [only] meet in thoughts and fancies. . . . My dear, if I can't write to you, I shall always think of you telling me things in your room at Rounton." Henceforth Bell would be less flamboyant in her solitude; indeed, sometimes she felt desperate. "I have cut the thread that binds us here to the outer world. I can hear no more from you or from anyone." When she penned those words to Charles, Gertrude was in deepest Arabia. In the early days of 1914 she had headed, along with a few Arab guides, into the Nejd desert. On February 26 she arrived at Ha'il, capital of the Rashid clan, who immediately threw her in prison for espionage—an accusation that, given what we know of Bell, was perhaps not without foundation.

"I should say the future lies with Ibn Sa'ud," she wrote with intelligent foresight when leaving the region. Bell was a political

Pages 108 and 109: Charles Doughty-Wylie in the garden of the British Consulate in Konya, Turkey, in May 1907; and Gertrude Bell as a student, c. 1888.

Facing page: Gertrude Bell and Fattuh in Turkey, June 1907; Bell in Baghdad.

Above: The archaeologist measuring the walls of a palace during a dig at Ukhaydir, Iraq, in March 1909.

Above: Bell and Faisal ibn Hussein, the king of Iraq, in 1922.

Facing page: Gertrude Bell posing with Winston Churchill on her right and Lawrence of Arabia on her left, during a conference in Cairo in 1921; portrait of Gertrude Bell in 1900.

animal, which is why archaeology was not fully satisfying to her, and why she never totally immersed herself in the desert, the way Isabelle Eberhardt had done. Even in Bedouin tents she remained an Oxford graduate and a Foreign Office creature. World War I would provide her with the opportunity to exercise her real talents by resolutely freeing her from the category of "eccentric traveler." It also freed her from the deep depression trigger by the death of Charles Doughty-Wylie, who fell in the Dardanelles in April 1915. "And if you die, wait for me," she wrote to him in her last letter. "I am not afraid of that other crossing; I will come to you."

In December 1915, Bell left for Cairo at the request of David Hogarth, who was charged with organizing military intelligence among the Arab tribes. There she met a young officer who resembled her like a twin: T. E. Lawrence. They were involved in a strategy of undermining the Ottoman government, which had allied itself to Germany. Assigned a mission as part of this project, Bell left for Baghdad to exploit the network of contacts she had built up during her archaeological expeditions. She went from Bedouin camp to camp, first locating the best interlocutor and then explaining, demonstrating, arguing, and calling on the pride and freedom of these masters of the desert, promising them rewards, constantly negotiating. The initialed signature she placed at the bottom of her reports, GLB, is well known to historians of the British intelligence service. Her greatest success was a treaty signed with the chief of the Anaizah tribe, who agreed to harass the Turks to the benefit of Great Britain.

The armistice found the adventurer and secret agent busier than ever: the politicians who were carving up the Ottoman Empire needed "advisers" of the caliber of Lawrence and Bell, even if they didn't always listen to their advice. Bell, like Lawrence, became more committed than ever, for she felt that only a British mandate could maintain peace in the Middle East. That is why she strongly supported Faisal, son of the sherif of Mecca, who wanted an autonomous kingdom to be created for his benefit. Not everyone appreciated the conspicuous female agent who tried to rally all of Baghdad to her protégé's cause. "If you can find a job for Miss Bell at home," wrote her hierarchical superior in Baghdad, Colonel Wilson, to his own superiors, "I think you would be well advised to do so. Her irresponsible activities are a source of considerable concern to me here and are not a little resented by the Political Officers."

But Bell reckoned she could do without her boss, given her well-placed connections. Soon Colonel Wilson was transferred, and his replacement in Baghdad was favorable to Faisal—Bell found herself more influential than ever. In August 1921, following a plebiscite organized by the British, Faisal was named king of a new nation, Iraq. "You may rely upon one thing," wrote Bell to her family, "I'll never engage in creating kings again; it's too great a strain." But she hardly meant it, for very soon she was missing the political activity. She might have enjoyed a well-earned rest, weary from years of fighting and what would now be called "lobbying." Yet she couldn't stand retirement, much less the feeling that the man she had put in power could do without her advice. The proud solitude

Above: Gertrude Bell organized a meeting between Abdel Aziz ibn Saud (the future king of Saudi Arabia) and British diplomat Sir Percy Cox in Mesopotamia, March 1901; Gertrude Bell in Babylon, April 1909.

Facing page: T. E. Lawrence and Gertrude Bell in Cairo.

with which she had so carefully cloaked herself slowly began to smother her, as did the torrid Mesopotamian summer. "I don't know what to do with myself of an afternoon," she confessed as summer began in 1926. Everyone advised her to return to her family in cool, leafy England. But Bell knew herself well enough to realize that she no longer had a place there. On July 11 she took an overdose of sleeping pills and never awoke. The only friend who still regularly visited her said it was probably suicide, but no letter or explanation was ever found. The best guess is that Bell of Baghdad didn't want to leave the Orient. Ever.

Already I want the next thing

The adventure always leaves one with a feeling of disillusion— don't you know it. . . .Dust and ashes in one's hand, dead bones that look as if they would never rise and dance—it's all nothing, and one turns away from it with a sigh, and tries to fix one's eyes on the new thing before one. This adventure hasn't been successful either, I haven't done what I meant to do. But I have got over that now. It's all done, and I don't care. Already I want the next thing, whatever it may be—I've done with that.

Letter to Charles Doughty-Wylie, March 1914, on returning from the expedition to Ha'il; quoted in Harry V.F. Winstone, *Gertrude Bell* (London: Jonathan Cape, 1978).

One fine spring day
in the late 1970s a strange
ceremony was held
in the archive vault of Castle
Museum in Norwich, England.
A small group of men solemnly
proceeded to open an old
japanned chest that had remained
closed since 1940. The sealed
chest bore the instructions:
"Not to be opened until
April 15, 1978."

Margaret Fountaine

Butterflies and Men

As mysterious as the object was, the gentlemen present seemed rather bored—they hardly expected to find a treasure, and in fact were only moderately intrigued by the contents once the chest was opened: twelve bound volumes, filled with writing in a regular, sloping hand, every now and then interspersed with postcards, dried flowers, and drawings. Indeed, this modest deposit hardly merited all the secrecy surrounding it, a condition demanded by the author. But the secrecy also conveyed the essence of her personality, for Margaret Fountaine was an eternal teenager, one who still kept a diary at age sixty-nine, after she had become a proper spinster (if plagued by a few shortcomings hard to reconcile with Victorian conventions). Romantic, she fell hopelessly in love with the most unsuitable men; brave and enterprising, she declared her love without hesitation; puritanical, she had no intention of yielding to love unless she was married. She embodied a combination of sensuality and strictness that once again seems so British.

Fountaine's first "fiancé" was a drunken, penniless Irishman. The young woman was aged twenty-two at the time. The daughter of a country clergyman near Norwich, raised by a mother who could never imagine herself going out without a chaperon even after eight pregnancies, Fountaine differed from her parents in so far as she never feared ridicule. She therefore pursued her Irishman for a number of years, even following him to Ireland. His resistance finally overcome, the young man at last promised to marry her—only to vanish, to the Fountaine family's great relief.

It was to console herself for this disappointment that Fountaine took her first voyage, in 1891. The trip was perfectly uneventful, yet determining: "I had lived all these years and never known till now

"Home sweet Home."

78. Cuban landscape. Paisaje Cubano.

Firenze
14/3/03 - Panorama dal Piazzale Michelangelo

Paul Trabert, Firenze-Lipsia 125

POSTAL CARD
Cuba

Sr. Arnaldo Ghista
Avenida de Mayo 1373
Buenos Aires
Argentina

Athen mit Akropolis.
Athens.
Athènes.

Pages 116 and 117: On April 15 every year, Margaret Fountaine began a new diary, in which she inserted a portrait of herself. These are two of those portraits.

Above: Postcards from Jamaica, Florence, Cuba, and Athens.

Facing page: A plate of illustrations from Cassell's *Book of European Butterflies*.

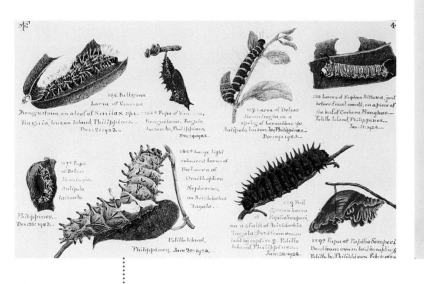

The handwritten diary pages contain the following text (right page):

his arms around me, I loved to see his eyes dilating and his chest heaving, and to feel the intensity of his passion; but when he asked me if I cared for him as he cared for me, I turned away, and did not hesitate to tell him that I did not, while in my heart I felt that I never would. And only two days after we were engaged I struggled to free myself, but it was only to draw the web more tightly round me, for how could I treat him thus? "I have not changed," he said very sadly, "but if you wish it for your pleasure I will say that I have." And I said there was but one way to extricate myself from this net into which I had fallen, and that was to break through its meshes; but should I ever have the heart to do it? So the matter drifted on. I could often have wished he was not quite so coarse in his words and actions, one thing he would always say was: "I love very much your legs." Then another day he would encircle my knees with his arm and say, "How are the legs?" "Oh they are all right thanks!" I used to reply laughing; but I never quite understood what he meant by this. However I did my best to raise the tone of his mind, though it seemed difficult to make him see that the animal side of human nature was not all we had to live for, or indeed the best part of it; but I did know there was a lot of good in the man and I felt it would very much depend upon me what he was eventually. I made him a present of an Arabic Bible and in return he made me a promise always to read it. I doubt if he has found the morality of the Old Testament altogether edifying and I have often wished that it had only been the New Testament with the doctrines of Christ, that I had given him. Of course my manner to him was very different now we were engaged I treated him more as an equal, and I was much less unkind. Was it possible after my long, rough stormy life, I had at last found one who would

WHITE JESSAMINE.

These were the first flowers given to me by Khalil Neimy after we were engaged. Baalbek, Syria. June 1901.

Above: Excerpts from Margaret Fountaine's diaries.

Facing page: Fountaine in Palm Springs with American entomologist Hal Newcombe.

how beautiful was this earth," she confided to her dear diary. With an amorousness that matched her wanderlust, Fountaine went on to collect men and countries: Italy, Sicily, Hungary, Greece, Turkey, Syria, Lebanon, South Africa, Rhodesia, Virginia, Jamaica, India, Tibet, Australia, and elsewhere. This list may resemble a catalog of Baedeker travel guides but it actually entailed authentic adventures: she got lost in the African bush, leapt from a train that was about to derail, experienced an earthquake in Cuba, nearly died of malaria on several occasions, and so on. At the same time, she became more or less engaged to a doctor, an Italian baron, an Egyptian naval officer, and a Hungarian aristocrat, to mention only the most glamorous fiancés. All of them courted her; she was in love with every one; not one ever slipped the ring on her finger.

Fortunately for posterity, Miss Fountaine compounded her first two passions with a third, one that would earn her a mention in the catalogs of various museums and institutes. In addition to men and foreign lands, she loved butterflies. From 1894 onward, the butterfly hunter never left home without her net. She hunted the *Magellanus* in the Philippines, the *Catagramma* in the Amazon, the *Agamemnon* in Africa, and *Lycaenidae* more or less everywhere. That was how she finally met a man with whom she shared her love—of butterflies. Khalil Neimy was a Syrian who already had a wife and children, alas, and thus could never lead Margaret to the altar. But at least he could be a trusty, loyal friend, who would travel with the English spinster for twenty-seven years. "Friend" is the accurate term, for nothing in

On her first meeting with Neimy, her inseparable companion for twenty-seven years:

It was late on a May afternoon when I found myself driving from the station in Damascus in company with three young Syrians; one a rather heavily-built man with round blue eyes, another a gray-eyed little man with a cunning smile and shifty glance—George and Elias Kaouam, proprietors of the Hotel Orient where I was to be received en pension for the modest sum of six francs a day. The fourth occupant of the carriage jogging us over the infamous roads into Damascus was slight, and instead of the sleek, well-fed appearance of the other two he had a crushed, almost cowed look; though his hair was quite fair his eyebrows and lashes and his moustache were dark, and it was almost a boyish face beneath the tarboosh which he wore thrown far back, the other two having theirs drawn down low over their foreheads. All I thought as I looked at this man for the first time was that he was very fair for a Syrian, and I liked to see a really fair man for a change. I noticed that his gray eyes were always looking toward me.

Extract from Margaret Fountaine, *Love among the Butterflies: The Travels and Adventures of a Victorian Lady* (London: William Collins & Sons, 1980).

her diary suggests that the two butterfly hunters ever went beyond the flirtation stage.

Their liaison nevertheless bore great fruit. The collection that Neimy and Fountaine jointly assembled is now one of the finest in the world. Even after Neimy's death in 1928, nothing could stop Fountaine's productive travels. At the age of seventy she was still able to ride some forty miles a day for the pleasure of capturing a rare specimen. It took a heart attack to put an end to her career—she died at the age of seventy-eight, net in hand, on the island of Trinidad.

What remains of her is simultaneously fragile and immutable: twenty-two thousand butterflies stored in ten mahogany cabinets, bequeathed to the Castle Museum in Norwich. Not to mention her diaries, whose value increases with each passing year.[1]

$\mathcal{D}$aisy Bates was a liar. She lied about her birth (which she claimed was noble), about her immigration to Australia (as a lady's companion, so she said), about her marriage to an alleged heir to a vast Australian estate, and so on. There is nevertheless one incontrovertibly true assertion in her biography: she spent forty years living in a tent on the edge of the desert among Australia's Aboriginal people.

Daisy Bates

Inventing a Life for Herself

Given the scope of such an adventure, the details of her background suddenly seem insignificant. She was in fact of modest birth, for records have been uncovered of her time in a Dublin orphanage and her marriage to a cowboy.[1] Or rather, two cowboys, since two marriage certificates have come to light, but no divorce decree. It would therefore seem that Bates married two different men in the space of eleven months—the existence of the first husband was never mentioned to the second (or to anyone else, for that matter).

In any case, from beyond the grave Bates might well retort that in Australia in those days—she landed there in 1880—everyone lied about their past. Or rather, a goodly number did, particularly among the émigrés from Great Britain and Ireland driven out by poverty or scandal. It was highly tempting for anyone launching a brand new life to reinvent the old one.

It hardly matters. The life of Daisy Bates, née O'Dwyer, really began in 1905, when she left the city of Perth, in southwestern Australia, and headed for the wilderness of the interior. It was while carrying out a philanthropic mission organized by a Catholic bishop, Monsignor Dean Martelli, that she fell in love with Aboriginal peoples. It was a strange encounter between an immigrant in search of a new life and people who, at that time, were considered at best a wretched vestige of the stone age and at worst a subhuman species whose rapid elimination was desirable.

Bates would remain among those people permanently. She who had constantly reinvented her past suddenly made a commitment that was absolute. Nothing could have predicted such a twist in her fate, yet she set up a camp at Eucla, on the vast desert plain of

Pages 122 and 123: An old aboriginal man teaching his son how to use a hunting spear in the Gibson Desert, Australia; and a photo of Daisy Bates in 1936.

Above: Bates with her camel-drawn buggy in Australia.

Facing page: Bates with a group of Aboriginal people in Broome, Australia, in 1899.

Nullarbor on the south coast, and began a new life. Her belongings consisted of a simple tent, a few provisions, a metal box for her papers—and a trunk full of dresses, hats, gloves, and parasols, because she still wanted to greet visitors with her old image: clean, stylish, distinguished. Her beauty, which was striking even beyond the age of forty, did not prevent her Aboriginal friends from calling her "Grandmother," because she adopted the role of caring for them at a time when syphilis raged among the population.

Bates was more than a nurse. She participated in ceremonies, festivities, and learned the Aboriginal language and religion. Soon she was so keen on Aboriginal culture that the Australian government financed her higher education. Within a matter of years anthropologists the world over were turning to her for information that they couldn't find themselves. One of the most distinguished of them, A. R. Radcliffe-Brown, would publish her results under his own name, failing to credit a source that he felt to be nothing more than an insignificant little lady.

Bates remained at her Eucla camp for sixteen years, years that slowly but surely brought her renown. She was recognized everywhere, both by whites for her knowledge and her commitment, and by Aboriginals for her skills as a carer and for her simple, warm way of minimizing differences. In March 1914 she was invited to the British Association for the Advancement of Science in Adelaide; determined to get there under her own steam, she and two companions traveled over six hundred miles on a buggy pulled by a camel.

Croup des fêmmes aborigines converties
à Broome, Ouest Australie.

Aboriginal Camp, Lake Way.

ABORIGINAL CAMP, W.A.

Above: The people of Lake Way, Australia, in 1900.

Facing page: Daisy Bates flanked by Aboriginal people.

Pages 128 and 129: The royal train used by the Duke of Gloucester during his trip across the Nullarbor plain, Australia (November 14, 1934).

Her baggage included silk undergarments, a blue silk dress, and a flowery hat that she intended to wear when she mounted the podium to denounce the imminent death of what she henceforth called "her people."

In 1919, she shifted camp. Her tent and trunkful of dresses were taken to Ooldea, a point on along the trans-Australian railway, in the same end-of-the-world landscape that she had known at Nullarbor—sand dunes, ghost towns, and unlikely train stations in the middle of nowhere. It was so parched that several years could go by without a drop of rain.

There were so few whites in Ooldea that Bates soon found herself invested with the office of justice of the peace, along with her role of nurse and official anthropologist. Such titles altered nothing of her everyday life that revolved around medical care, social work,

and outside visits—from journalists, academics, civil servants. In 1934, over seventy years old, she was made a Commander of the Order of the British Empire and an adviser on Aboriginal Affairs in Canberra. After a long stay in Adelaide for the publication of her book, *The Passing of the Aborigines,* she returned to her camp at Ooldea, which she only left in 1945, due to health problems. In 1948 a reporter set out to find her and stubbornly tracked her down, even though his initial inquiries about her were met with the response that she had died long ago. He found her in a little bungalow in Adelaide, where she received him dressed in the same suit she wore in 1905, parasol in hand. She died in 1951, aged eighty-eight if the birth date on her tombstone is to be believed. A few months later, the last Aboriginal residents of the Nullarbor plain were evacuated to make room for nuclear testing.

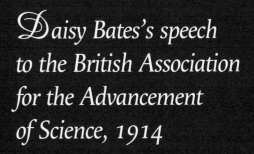

Daisy Bates's speech to the British Association for the Advancement of Science, 1914

Do any of you realize what has been happening along the Line? How girls of ten years old or even younger are stolen from their families and raped and maltreated by gangs of white men and then thrown out like so much rubbish? Do you know how fast syphilis can take hold of a body and how it makes a person stink of decay? I have watched so many young men and young women come in from the desert shining and naked and then within such a short time I have buried them. . . .

If any of you lived close to the Line, as I have done for the last sixteen years, then you would know how dangerous the low whites can be and I am sure you would be horrified by their savagery and brutality just as I have been. I am so glad you invited me to speak to you because it restores my faith in justice and the British Empire; a faith which I must admit has been a little shaken recently. Now Kabbarli will look after her people like a shepherd with his flock and when they are ready she will open the doors for them so that those who want to enter the world of railway trains and big cities can do so, while the rest are free to stay.

Quoted in Julia Blackburn,
Daisy Bates in the Desert,
(London: Vintage Books, 1995).

Nellie Bly's most famous voyage almost seems like a joke: in the year 1889 she wagered, with a smile, that she could beat Phileas Fogg's record. Even the accoutrements she ordered for the trip seemed like a put-on—a long, checked coat, a small leather traveling bag, and an umbrella. Miss Bly wanted to be a caricature of the caricatured English protagonist of Frenchman Jules Verne's famous novel.

Nellie Bly

Around the World in Seventy-Two Days

However, it is perhaps unfortunate that the joke stuck to her image so tenaciously. Bly was much more than the pretty American woman sitting astride a crescent moon, as popularized by her "travel cards."

Her career began at the age of eighteen. In reply to an editorial that she felt was misogynist, she wrote an anonymous letter to the *Pittsburgh Dispatch* signed "Lonely Orphan Girl." Although she had indeed lost her father years before, she was hardly an orphan or lonely. Born Elizabeth Cochrane but nicknamed "Pink" for her love of dresses in that color, she had a mother, a step father (whom she hated), and many brothers and sisters (whose education she partly assumed). One thing was undeniably true: she knew how to write. Thus the managing editor of the *Pittsburgh Dispatch* published an ad asking the Lonely Orphan Girl, with her strong journalistic bent, to come forward and identify herself. Cochrane did so, and subsequently became a correspondent for the newspaper under the byline "Nellie Bly," from a popular song of the day. She specialized in social journalism, describing the conditions of female factory workers, the impact of marital laws on women's lives, and so on. But the employers of these working women then threatened to cease advertising in the *Pittsburgh Dispatch,* at which point Bly was assigned less risky stories on gardening, cooking, and fashion.

She didn't stick with those subjects for long. She resigned and went to Mexico, where she wrote articles on corruption and poverty, until she was deported by the Mexican government.

Bly felt it was impossible to return to Pittsburgh, so she headed for New York. And since she was confident of her talent, she set her sights on the *New York World*, the well-known newspaper published by Joseph Pulitzer. She finally managed to get an interview, and her

Pages 130 and 131: Workers at the General Electric Company in Schenectady, New York, 1904; a photo of Nellie Bly in travel dress, 1888.

Above: Wood engraving of an asylum on Blackwell's Island, New York, in 1898; a portrait of the reporter two years later.

Facing page: American express train, 1853; and a postcard from Port Said, Egypt.

first story for the paper was an investigation into a women's mental asylum, which won the respect of her editor. Pulitzer liked the type of journalism that alarmed editors in Pittsburgh, and he realized his paper could benefit from the impact made by this woman who was afraid of nothing. That is why, when she became indignant at the idea that a male reporter was to be given the assignment to travel around the world faster than Phileas Fogg, he allowed her to take up the challenge of beating Verne's hero at his own game.

She set sail on November 14, 1889, and traveled freely by boat, train, bus, and rickshaw, focusing mainly on timetables and reservations, unrewarding tasks that are nevertheless crucial to any adventure, then as now. When she was not racing from station to port, the journalist dashed off a daily bulletin for readers of the *New York World,* which she filled with picturesque incidents—all of which took place on one mode of transportation or another. For Nellie's world was one of passengers—all nomadic, all caught between two continents or two cities, wrestling with their trunks and with the boredom of travelers waiting to arrive. But the reporter's eye was so sharp and her pen so swift that the daily chronicle became a serial eagerly awaited by all New Yorkers. So much so, that when this American Phileas Fogg set foot once more on the docks of Manhattan—seventy-two days, eleven minutes, and seven seconds after setting out—she was met by fireworks, a parade, and bands.

In the end, Nellie got what she wanted. Although her voyage brought her little more than champagne corks in the air, the fame it

AMERICAN EXPRESS TRAIN.

NEW YORK, PUBLISHED BY CURRIER & IVES, 152 NASSAU ST.

Port-Said
Port

won her allowed her to write freely about the subjects that really mattered to her: corruption, the condition of unwed mothers, workers, and domestic servants, and so on. Even before Jack London thought of disguising himself as a railroad worker, Bly passed herself off as a maid the better to describe the life of servants.

Bly's courage didn't end at the tip of her pen. After a ten-year marriage to a millionaire industrialist from Catskill, New York, she was widowed, and found herself owner of the Iron Clad Manufacturing Company. She could have enjoyed her income quietly, but she decided instead to reform the factory: she did away with piecework, she built a recreation center for the workers, and she established hunting and fishing clubs, a library, and other facilities. Alas, Bly was more skilled at journalism than industrial management and she went bankrupt. Having sailed to England to escape her creditors, she found herself caught in Europe when World War I broke out. No matter: she picked up her old skills and became a war correspondent. She made a living from this work until 1919. Then she returned to New York, where she devoted most of her articles for the *New York Evening Journal* to the issue of abandoned children. She died of pneumonia on January 27, 1922, aged just fifty-eight, hailed by all American newspapers as a great figure in journalism.

NELLIE BLY., BYE AND BYE.

"O bye and bye," dreams Nellie Bly,
Along a strand of light I'll hie;
And stars and gleams will follow too,
But they must hustle if they do."

USE
Dr. Morse's Indian Root Pills,
for Biliousness, Headache, and Constipation.

NELLIE BLY, ON THE FLY.

When Nellie Bly went on the fly,
To show what courage dared to try,
She made the startled world contess:
Men don't monopolize success.

Smoke the popular
"LA CIGALE" CIGAR
O. F. RAWSON & CO., MFRS.

Above and facing page:
Nellie Bly "travel cards"; and a portrait photo.

And a jar of cold cream

I have been asked very often since my return how many changes of clothing I took in my solitary hand-bag. Some have thought I took but one; others think I carried silk which occupies but little space, and others have asked if I did not buy what I needed at the different ports. One never knows the capacity of an ordinary hand-satchel until dire necessity compels the exercise of all one's ingenuity to reduce every thing to the smallest possible compass. In mine I was able to pack two traveling caps, three veils, a pair of slippers, a complete outfit of toilet articles, ink-stand, pens, pencils, and copy-paper, pins, needles and thread, a dressing gown, a tennis blazer, a small flask and a drinking cup, several complete changes of underwear, a liberal supply of handkerchiefs and fresh ruchings and most bulky and uncompromising of all, a jar of cold cream to keep my face from chapping in the varied climates I should encounter.

That jar of cold cream was the bane of my existence. It seemed to take up more room than everything else in the bag and was always getting into just the place that would keep me from closing the satchel. Over my arm I carried a silk waterproof, the only provision I made against rainy weather. After-experience showed me that I had taken too much rather than too little baggage. At every port where I stopped at I could have bought anything from a ready-made dress down, except possibly at Aden, and as I did not visit the shops there I cannot speak from knowledge.

Nellie Bly, *Around the World in Seventy-Two Days* (New York: The Pictorial Weekly Company, 1890).

Although many woman adventurers set out from comfortable nests, the opposite was true of Isabelle Eberhardt. She came from nowhere, she had no single identity, and she was constantly trying to assemble the fragmented parts of her personality and find a single place to house them. And when she finally found that place, she drowned in it.

Despite her multiple identities, Eberhardt had no name at birth. That is to say, she was given her mother's name, which in 1877 meant not having one.

Isabelle Eberhardt

Drowning in the Desert

Her mother was the German–Russian widow of a Russian aristocrat; her father was the family tutor, a defrocked Orthodox priest who was both a scholar and an anarchist. Born in Geneva, Switzerland, Eberhardt was raised by her father, who refused to recognize her but who brought her up with strict respect for principles that were rigorously unconventional—indeed, tyrannically unconventional. Over the years, the utopian household increasingly came to resemble a prison, and the spirit of liberty that the anarchist inculcated not only in his daughter but also in the widow's legitimate sons and daughter slowly turned against him: all the children fled from him one after the other, either by running away or committing suicide.

Isabelle was one of those who ran away. Her first escape route was epistolary. For three years, from age seventeen to twenty, she entered into intense correspondence with various people she either knew (such as her half-brother, who had enlisted in the French Foreign Legion) or didn't know (such as a young French officer stationed in Algeria, whose address she obtained from a classified ad). Such escapism could hardly help a young woman in search of her own identity. Her father had already encouraged her to dress as a man, and now she began signing her letters with pseudonyms that were sometimes male, sometimes female, and variously Russian, French, Arab, and so on.

Eberhardt would have to cross the Mediterranean in order to begin pulling her fragmented personality together. The trip to North Africa had been anticipated for so long that it represented a culmination rather than a sudden impulse. She had first been introduced to the Arab world by her father, who spoke and wrote Arabic; then by her brother's Turkish friend, who had initiated her into Islam, a religion

75 BISKRA. — Rue des Ouleds-Naïls et Cafés Maures. — LL.

that accorded with the radical rejection of the West in which Eberhardt had been steeped during childhood; and finally she answered an ad published by a Paris-based teacher of Arabic and enthusiastically continued her education by correspondence (passing herself off as one Nicolas Podorovski). She was twenty in 1897 when she convinced her mother to accept an invitation from a friend who had moved to the city of Bône (present-day Annaba) in Algeria. Even before boarding the boat, Eberhardt felt that her true home was over there, in the shade of the mosques.

In a matter of weeks she had left her friend's European household, moved into the Arab quarter, and converted to Islam—then persuaded her mother to do the same. She swapped her European garb for that of an Arab horseman, and when her mother died of a heart attack six months later, she had the tombstone carved with her mother's Arabic name, Fatima Manubia. Eberhardt then experienced a bout of depression—which would become an all-too-familiar event—and began drinking alcohol. At the same time, from the very depths of melancholy, she made positive steps toward self-knowledge and the affirmation of her independence. The character she adopted in public, forged in sorrow, would become her authentic identity over the years, ousting all the others: she was seen dressed in a long white burnoose, hair cut short, wandering among the poorer quarters or sitting for a long time in shadowy cafés, smoking kef and discussing theology and poetry.

Eberhardt then took this character further and further, deep into Algeria, to the edges of the Sahara. She increasingly embraced, in a non-provocative way, the very ambiguity of her character, which

Oran 4 mars 1901
Reçu vos 3 cartes et surtout celle nous donnant l'image de nos agréables correspondants.
Merci, Madame, ce sont bien les bonnes figures que font deviner vos agréables correspondances.
Oui, il faudra que je vous adresse des cartes d'Alger car je suis un peu embarrassé avec Oran. Comptez aussi sur un envoi prochain de nos photographies. Je suis un peu honteux de mêler l'aîné d'avance.
Recevez Madame l'assurance de nos meilleurs sentiments.
E. Meynard

Sahara Algérien. — Palmiers, Régimes de Dattes. — ND Phot

the more conventional of the people she met on her route found hard to understand.

Fortunately for Eberhardt, she also encountered other men and women who realized that her disguise—"a tall, young, androgynous man"—and her suicidal tendency cloaked a profound philosophy and sensibility that went far beyond the cheap Orientalism that, to certain eyes, she may have incarnated. Foremost among these people were the author Victor Barrucand (who was living in Algeria), the travel writer Lydie Paschkoff (herself an intrepid wanderer known for her erudition),¹ and, later, General Lyautey (military commander of the region). The real tragedy of Eberhardt's life was probably the fact that even her most enlightened friends were more interested in her character than her writings. "Spend a year in Paris," advised Lydie Paschkoff in a letter, "and everywhere you go, you must wear elegant Oriental dress. Abu will tell you how much his costume helped him to become fashionable." But Eberhardt wanted to be a writer—one full of doubt and humility, perhaps, but a writer above all.

Throughout the year 1900, while experimenting with short tales of travel—half-fictional, half-journalistic pieces that remain her finest writing—the writer henceforth called Si Mahmoud Saadi became ever more nomadic: from El Oued to Batna, then to Marseille and Geneva (where she vainly hoped to receive money from the sale of her mother's house), on to Sardinia, finally back to El Oued.

Despite a lack of funds, despite bouts of malaria, Eberhardt thought she would remain in southern Algeria forever. But one encounter dictated otherwise: she fell in love with a *spahi*, or native cavalryman in

Pages 136 and 137: Postcard of the docks at Abbona, Algeria; and a photo of Isabelle Eberhardt aged seventeen.

Facing page, clockwise: Postcard of Biskra, Algeria; a Moorish coffee house in Algeria; and a portrait of Eberhardt aged eighteen.

Above: Postcard of the Algerian Sahara.

TÉNÈS.— Commune mixte. Les bureaux   Edit. Monneret

Above: Postcard of Ténès.

Facing page: The 1904 flood at Ain Sefra
that killed Eberhardt; and her tomb.

the French army, named Slimène Mehmi. She created a scandal by
pursuing him, by being seen publicly with him, and by convincing him
to sneak her into the Qadriya religious confraternity, where she learned
Sufi techniques for attaining mystical ecstasy. The scandal grew all the
louder when she became the target of a failed assassination attempt, probably committed by a rival confraternity. On January 29, 1901, the French
authorities deported her and she was forced to leave Slimène.

By this time, Eberhardt experienced her deportation as a true
exile, for she felt she had become permanently Algerian. In
Marseille, she struggled to obtain authorization to marry Slimène
Mehmi—she was a Muslim and she was pro-French, she argued, so
why keep her apart from the man she loved, an Algerian officer in
the French army? Her persistence and her friends finally got the
better of the French bureaucracy: on October 17, 1901, she married
her *spahi,* then helped him pass the test to become an army inter-
preter, which would lead to a posting in Algeria on acceptable
financial terms. By early 1902 the couple had settled in Ténès,
roughly 120 miles from Algiers. Eberhardt, however, was already
growing restless. The life of an officer's wife was unsatisfying; soon
she was discarding the blue jacket she had agreed to wear as a
minimal sign of respect for colonial society. Once again she donned
her burnoose and began wandering down the shadowy streets of the
Arab quarter, drinking absinthe and smoking with chance companions. Then she began writing regularly for the Arabic newspaper
Akhbar. Scandal flared up once again—the French community in
Algeria didn't like this hybrid creature that scuttled between two

Aïn-Séfra — À la recherche des victimes de la catastrophe

17. - AIN-SEFRA. - Tombeau de Isabelle Eberhart, Épouse Ehnaf Slimane, morte à 27 ans dans la catastrophe de Aïn Sefra, le 11 octobre 1904

worlds. Soon a rival newspaper claimed that she was stirring up the native population (later, the Algerians would accuse her of having spied for the French army). Such was the outcry that Slimène had to resign his post; once again it took an intervention on the part of her friends before she could continue her ambiguous existence in peace.

This time the friends were in high places: in September 1903, Eberhardt met General Louis Lyautey, an advocate of "gentle" colonization that favored coming to terms with the locals rather than imposing the force of arms. Eberhardt and Lyautey both envisaged a melting-pot society, and the general fell under the charm of this strange woman who seemed to be the offspring of a marriage between East and West. She was not truly at peace, however, and was even doomed in certain respects, for Eberhardt capitulated, without fighting back, to the demons that devoured her—alcohol, kef, syphilis.

It is probable that even if Isabelle Eberhardt had not drowned in a flash flood that swept through the town of Ain Sefra on October 21, 1904, she would have had a hard time making it to thirty. Some people later wrote that it was her Rimbaud-style destiny to remain eternally young. A loss is nevertheless keenly felt on reading her final texts, never published during her lifetime, written in southern Algeria and rescued from the mud by Victor Barrucand. "Recent days have ticked by, monotonous. Prostrate under a cloudless sky, Algiers dozes. The streets, where passersby are few, seem wider, while swarms of blue flies buzz in the squat shadows of the houses"[2]

It is a shame, in any case, that this twenty-seven-year-old writer was unable to continue her journey.

The hermaphrodite

She drank too much, which was the only thing that clashed with her profound acceptance of the Muslim faith. Indeed, she was intensely religious. Made of the stuff of mystics and martyrs. . . . She lived like a man or boy, because physically she was less girl than boy. She had a hermaphroditic appearance; she was passionate and sensual, but not like a woman. Her chest was completely flat. She had her little vanities—those of an elegant Arab man. Her fine hands were always henna'd, her burnoose was always spotless, and when she had the means she drenched herself in those strong scents that all Arab men love. . . .

During certain periods she would spent entire days in the souks; when she saw a man she desired, she took him. She just nodded at him and they would leave together. She was never a hypocrite, never tried to hide her affairs. And why would she, in any case? It was just another side of her character. She also experienced, I believe, profound religious ecstasies—but those, she hid.

Account by an acquaintance in Ténès, quoted in Eglal Errara, *Isabelle Eberhardt, Lettres et journaliers* (Paris: Actes Sud, 1987).

141

Some adventures happen
only when the two halves
of a single entity come together.
Such was the cruise of the *Snark*.
The first half of the entity was Jack
London. In 1900, the twenty-four-
year-old adventure writer was
already famous. His charm and his
experiences had earned him success
of every kind, but he still felt
unfulfilled at that point.
His mind was still unsettled,
in a whirl, and he was restless
for action and stimulation.

Charmian Kittredge

"Why wait five years?"

He spent more than he earned, he drank too much, and he got into fights. His wife, Bess London, couldn't take it any more, and retreated into motherhood and a social circle too restrictive for the doe-eyed giant she had married.

The second half of the entity was Charmian Kittredge. Unlike Bess, this twenty-nine-year-old woman had not retreated into anything—ever. Born in 1871, she had been raised by a strong-willed aunt who advocated free love, socialism, feminism, and vegetarianism. Charmian was the highly successful product of an unconventional education. In the mid-1880s she went swimming, riding, and played the organ. She loved singing at the top of her lungs and she sat astride the saddle when she rode. Above all, she was proud of having a true profession. Already she had paid for her own education by working as a secretary for the owners of Mills Academy, thanks to the training in typing and stenography that her aunt had urged her to acquire. Employed by a San Francisco shipper, she proudly rode the horse that her salary had enabled her to buy on her own, at the age of only nineteen. Soon she began publishing her first articles, including a favorable review of *The Son of the Wolf*, by a certain Jack London. When deep feelings arose between the adventure writer and the fearless woman, leading to a secret affair, their friends were unanimous in saying that Jack and Charmian were made for each other.

One day in 1905 London began to daydream with the woman who was to become his second wife. "What do you say, Charmian?—suppose five years from now, after we're married and have built our house somewhere, we start on a voyage around the world in a forty-five-foot yacht."

Pages 142 and 143: Charmian Kittredge and Jack London on the porch of their house in the United States on January 1, 1900; and a portrait of Charmian Kittredge.

Above: Young Hawaiian woman in traditional dress, Honolulu, 1920; Melanesian canoes; and Tulagi Bay, Solomon Islands.

Facing page: Kittredge in 1922.

To which Charmian replied, "Why wait five years? I love a boat, you love a boat; let's call the boat our house."

Thus they began building the *Snark*, a handsome forty-five-foot yacht whose construction schedule had to bend to London's irregular income—it was only in 1907 that she was finally put to sea.

The term "cruise" used by London to describe his crossing of the Pacific was an understatement. It was indeed a cruise that he thought he and Charmian would take when they sailed west. But right from week one, the *Snark* decided otherwise: hit by a barge in San Francisco Bay, it sprang a leak that damaged the engines and ruined the provisions in the hold. A long stopover in Honolulu was required to reorganize the voyage, hire a crew, and find their own sea legs. Finally, the *Snark* set sail again. After a nonstop crossing of sixty days, the couple began a long period of wandering among the archipelagoes of Polynesia and Melanesia. It was a tragicomic medley of navigation, literature, and human encounters that ultimately took them to Australia.

In those days, the Pacific isles in no way resembled the touristy clichés with which their names would later be associated: the Marquesas, Tahiti, Bora-Bora, Pago Pago, the Samoan Islands, Guadalcanal. Sure enough, coconut palms and native damsels were to be found there, but so were fevers and sores that never healed, damage to a jury-rigged ship, and total isolation in every sense of the term. Jack and Charmian managed to profit from each stopover, however, despite various attacks of tropical illnesses. Few characters

1922

and few landscapes escaped the sharp eye of the writer, who produced some of his best short stories in the overheated cabin of the *Snark*, scribbling away and dictating to Charmian, the former stenotypist.

Their curiosity was so unquenchable that they accepted the offer of a certain Captain Jansen to accompany them in a slave hunt disguised as a "recruitment drive for free laborers" that was still practiced in the Solomon Islands. In those latitudes, the Pacific was a place of obscurity and death. A few months earlier, Jansen's predecessor had been killed by cannibals on Mala Island. Charmian would describe the place thus: "Very curious and beautiful are these snug strongholds against man and nature, close-walled with firm masonry of coral blocks to resist the smashing sea, the straight lines of walls broken by thatched village roofs and the graceful bendings and sketchy angles of coconut palms. The openings for canoe landings are narrow and rough and steep, as if cannon had tumbled in a thick section of wall, the sides waving with ferns."[1] The two adventurers wondered if their career would come to an end right there: a gale drove Captain Jensen's ship onto a reef, and the surrounding waters were thick with canoes full of armed men who were waiting patiently until the disaster occurred and they could rush the wreck. Jack and Charmian set about gathering up their belongings, including manuscripts and typewriter, when after some four hours and the help of a passing ship, the slave hunter managed to refloat his vessel. From this incident London brought back a large terrier

Facing page, clockwise: The *Snark* leaving Honolulu, Oahu, for the island of Hawaii, August 15, 1907; Charmian and Jack sitting on the hull of their boat; Kittredge in riding dress, with her dog Possum.

Above: Charmian Kittredge and Jack London with the famous Remington No. 7 typewriter.

Above: Kittredge on the Solomon Islands; Carrie Sterling, Kittredge, James Hopper, George Sterling, and London on board the *Snark* in 1907.

Facing page: Jack and Charmian on Waikiki Beach, Hawaii, in 1915.

named Satan, who would become the protagonist of several tales, including *The Adventure.* The Solomon Islands were the *Snark*'s last port of call. Her skipper's health had so deteriorated that a hospital had to be found, fast. So the cruise came to an end and the couple returned to California to pursue a partnership in literature, on horseback, and under sail. One year before his death in 1915, London penned a dedication to Kittredge in a copy of *The Scarlet Plague*: "My Mate-Woman: And here, in blessed Hawaii eight years after our voyage here in our own speck boat, we find ourselves, not merely again, but more bound to each other than then or than ever. Mate Man."

Although five years older than Jack, Charmian outlived him by thirty-nine years. As free as she had always been, she willingly put all her energy into promoting London's œuvre, making trips and giving lectures so that his stories and novels could be republished and adapted for the screen. Probably it was an attempt to rediscover the passion of her youth that encouraged her to hitch up with the travel writer Frederick O'Brien, although she never remarried, despite several offers. She died in 1955, aged ninety-four. In a strange twist of fate, it was Kittredge who, in 1929, helped to finance the first trip taken by Ella Maillart, a young woman she met in Europe.

"on the BEach at Waikiki" — 1915

She laughed a great deal

Charmian had a genuine love for music, sang pleasingly, and even had the force and discipline to train herself to become an accomplished pianist. She ... laughed a great deal, even though the point of humor might be obscure, and was an indefatigable talker. She could carry on an intelligent and logical discussion, for she had a varied flow of words and phrases. A woman of great physical courage, she was the first to ride astride a horse into the hills when few women were riding at all.... Ambitious, both socially and intellectually, she worked hard to advance herself, and saved her money.

Irving Stone, *Jack London, Sailor on Horseback* (New York: Doubleday, 1938).

There is a paradox concerning the Western women who openly declared themselves to be followers of Buddhism in the early 1900s: almost all of them were intrepid women of action. Their public quest for release from desire and its concomitant suffering was the fruit of a devouring passion for freedom of thought and for a distinct individualism, characteristics that ill fit the sublime renunciation of self that their spiritual masters taught them.

Alexandra David-Néel

Lamp of Wisdom

Looking at the face of this fifty-five-year-old woman wearing Tibetan dress, astride a horse, it is hard not to be aware of this paradox—it is not serenity and enlightened wisdom that radiate from her furrowed wrinkles and straightforward gaze, but rather terrific willfulness and staunch determination.

Her Buddhist name was Lamp of Wisdom. The early period of her life might challenge the suitability of this choice of name. It was probably hard to behave "wisely" if you were daughter of an idealistic, free-thinking father and a devout, church-going mother, as suggested by young Alexandra's tendency to run away. At age seventeen she ran away from her home in Belgium to London; two years later she ran away again, this time to Switzerland, where her mother found her; another two years later, no longer a minor, she got as far as India, where she spent her modest heritage. Already she had studied music, voice, Buddhism, and Sanskrit. On her return, penniless, she tried to making a living as a opera singer, which took her to Hanoi, where a theater hired her to perform leading roles; her new career took her to Athens, Marseille, Tunis, and elsewhere, yet nevertheless left her enough time to throw herself totally into promoting women's causes, theosophy, and Orientalism.

Alexandra David not only liked action, she liked contradiction. That is why she took a lover but refused to marry him. And probably also why she ultimately wound up getting married when an unrepentant seducer, Philippe Néel, bluntly told her: "If you were to ask when we're getting married, I'd reply, 'Never!'" The challenge was too tempting for Alexandra: on August 4, 1904, she and Philippe were united for better or for worse, in Tunis.

After having been an opera singer, she became a lecturer and journalist, giving talks on Hinduism and publishing regularly on feminism. She addressed subjects such as "The Importance of Ambient Influences on a Philosophical Viewpoint" and yet continued to dispense her own ideas—at that time she was simultaneously espousing theosophy, Rosicrucianism, freemasonry, and Buddhism. She had thought she might be able to settle down if she became a proper middle-class wife, but the opposite occurred: she became unbearable both to her husband and herself. Dissatisfied, muddled, complaining, she wound up demanding that Philippe pay her a "salary," then made the decision to put an end to all sexual relations for the reason that therein lay, she claimed, the origins of all women's woes. "Remain a virgin!" would be the advice she henceforth gave her fellow females.

Even her departure for Asia sprang from motives that were not necessarily related to an idealistic quest. "There is a very honorable role to fill in French Orientalism," she wrote to her husband, "a role more visible and more interesting that that of our specialists. . . . Take the immense popularity of Bergson: excuse my boldness, but I think I have much more to say than he does. That, however, requires energy, work, and documentation that leaves no scope for criticism. When I am criticized by ivory-tower scholars, the public must be able to think, 'True, those people are well-known academics, but *she* has experienced things she's talking about, she has touched them and seen them first hand.'"

When it came to energy, Alexandra David-Néel clearly had too much. Only a voyage to the ends of the earth could assuage her hunger to act, to see, to understand, to discover. Thus she set out again in August 1911, with her husband's consent, which was still indispensable at that time. On April 12, 1912, she managed to approach the Dalai Lama—less to penetrate the secrets of the "middle way" than to satisfy her journalistic curiosity. She was still persisting in 1913: "I am dwelling on the wonderful dream of traveling to Lhasa. . . . of the fame that would follow." Yet, she corrected herself, "one must avoid desire, as Buddhism teaches, because desire is suffering." How she would suffer! For the desire was there, the desire that precedes action, and it led to suffering: in order to go to Lhasa, she first had to convince her husband to continue financing her—which he finally agreed to do. "In the end, the one who practiced renunciation was Philippe," noted David-Néel's biographer, Jean Chalon.[1]

After a long stay in Sikkim, then a longer one in Varanasi (Benares), David-Néel returned to Sikkim in May 1914. There she hired a servant named Yongden, who over the years would become her adopted son. David-Néel thus steadily took on her permanent persona of female lama, with her round silhouette wrapped in a vast Tibetan robe, her face marked by the mountain air, her gaze that betrayed the Western woman in disguise.

As war spread across Europe, David-Néel withdrew into a spiritual retreat that lasted nearly two years, conducted under the

Pages 150 and 151: The Potala Palace in Lhasa, Tibet; and a photo of Alexandra David-Néel.

Facing page, clockwise: Philippe and Alexandra in the former Arab palace on rue Abd'el Wahab, Tunis; Alexandra at her desk in Tunis, where she lived from 1904 to 1911; Alexandra as an opera singer.

Above: A review of troops in the streets of Chungking prior to their departure for the Sino-Japanese War in 1938; and the temple built by Rajah Amehti in Benares (Varanasi).

supervision of a spiritual mentor. "In India," she wrote to Philippe, "living in a cave is the standard certification of great yogis." Her cave was furnished with many carpets and knickknacks, yet David-Néel nevertheless managed to learn the secrets of Lamaism, meditation, and ecstasy, thereby earning her new name of Lamp of Wisdom. In July 1916 she felt ready to continue on the path that led to her true goal—being the first European woman to enter the forbidden city of Lhasa.

By then she knew Asia well enough to realize that it was pointless to try to enter Tibet from India. Thus, happily steeped in her adopted world—indifferent both to passing time and to the worldwide war—she left for Japan and then headed into Mongolia, finally crossing China at a modest pace, accepting hospitality from both Buddhist monasteries and Christian missionaries. Her face became increasingly weathered; more and more she resembled her own disguise of a wizened, pious old lady (though she never renounced her daily bath, despite the risk of giving herself away). Late in October 1923, aged fifty-five, twelve years after having left France, eight years after having been renamed Lamp of Wisdom by her yogi, she reached the border of Tibet, a land that foreigners were forbidden to enter by all authorities—Chinese, English, and Tibetan. More than one white had been imprisoned, indeed murdered, there. In order to avoid the same fate, David-Néel and Yongden never passed through villages in daytime, and they slept outdoors in all weather. They looked like beggars and, in fact, went begging.

Sometimes they traveled with pilgrims who mistook David-Néel for a native of Ladakh; sometimes they had nothing to eat but boiled leather. Finally, at the end of January 1924, Lamp of Wisdom entered the holy city "in a skeletal state." She remained there until April without being discovered; she managed to have her picture taken in front of the Potala Palace by a local photographer, to prove that her exploit was authentic. By early June she was back in India, where she found herself again in Western civilization—in the form of British colonialists—for the first time in twelve years. World War I had come to a close, and the Roaring Twenties were in full swing— David-Néel had difficulty hiding her scandalized stupefaction on seeing an Englishman without a tie, collar unbuttoned, legs completely bare except for what she called "underwear"—in fact, shorts—that "revealed the thighs of a gentlemen who seems so unlike one." It was almost as though David-Néel had fallen asleep in the nineteenth century and awakened in the twentieth. Her trip through time seemed more exotic than her voyage across Asia.

Facing page: On the border of Tibet and Yunnan, a village located on the sacred trail circling Kawa Karpo. As the Sino-Japanese War became imminent, David-Néel headed for Buddhist monasteries in the Wutai Shan range, 250 miles southwest of Beijing. On the back of this photograph, she wrote, "What remains of my luggage, Hankow, 1938." When fleeing to Hankow, she had indeed lost most of her baggage.

Above: David-Néel in Tibetan dress, with nuns from a small Chorten Nyima convent, at the foot of the Tibetan Himalayas, October 1914; a photo of David-Néel and Yongden, c. 1920–23, on the back of which she wrote, prior to sending it to Philippe, "a woman of Great Perfection of the Red Sect wearing a magic dagger at her waist and holding prayer beads of human bones in her hand, with a disciple behind her."

Above: David-Néel sitting in front of her retreat, *Dechen Ashram* ("hermitage of peace"), at 16,000 feet. She stayed there in the fall of 1914, then from summer 1915 to the following summer. David-Néel during her excursion to northern Sikkim in September 1914; on the back of the photo she wrote, "Camp at the foot of Tangchung Col. Photo taken prior to the departure of the Maharajah [Sidkeong Tulku of Sikkim] for Talung—I would never see him again!"

Facing page: Press clippings from 1924 and 1925.

At that point, Lamp of Wisdom had only one desire—to return to France and profit from her incredible adventure. She would not be disappointed. Fame awaited her everywhere in Europe and the United States. The whole world henceforth knew her as the "Parisian woman who got into Lhasa." Books, articles, lectures, medals, warm congratulations, and letters from admirers came in an avalanche that her health had difficulty withstanding.

Finally, in January 1937, even though she had bought a property in Digne, France, where she intended to spend the rest of her life—rich and famous—she left again for China and ultimately Tibet, fleeing the chaos that was then gripping the Far East. She would remain there until 1946, once again far from the rumble of war.

Despite her age, despite infirmity and fatigue, David-Néel's career was not yet over. She returned to her reporting, writing, and lecturing activities (publishing five books in three years), even as she tended her vegetable garden in Digne and corresponded with people the world over. The only pause in her frantic activity came following the death of Yongden, whom she called "my son," and who had been her partner in adventure for forty long years. David-Néel was eighty-seven years old at that point. "I don't think I'll outlive him by much," she wrote to a female correspondent, "nor do I desire to." She nevertheless lived for another fourteen years. Although confined to a wheelchair and deprived of the laughter of Yongden—the only man she really loved—she slowly returned to active life. In 1969, she made a point of renewing her passport before it expired. She was 101. She lived for another five months, until September of that year. Perhaps she had finally found wisdom.

completely as the most demanding person can imagine). This outing would have been considered most rugged for a young and healthy man; that a woman of my age would undertake it may have seemed pure folly, and yet I have pulled it off totally, although even if someone offered me a million francs to do it again in the same conditions I think I'd refuse. . . . I'll mention only that I arrived in Lhasa in a skeletal state. When I rub my hand over my body I find there is just thin skin covering my bones. . . . The most annoying thing is. . . my weakness, although I didn't notice it too much until now due to stimulants. I'll have to buck myself up, I'll have to sleep and eat for a good, long month once I'm out of Tibet, which won't be for another six weeks because there is still a long route from Lhasa to the border and then the entire Himalaya range has to be crossed.

Letter to Philippe Néel, written from Lhasa on (approximately) February 28, 1924, published in Alexandra David-Néel, *Journal de Voyage*, vol. 2 (Paris: Plon, 1976).

Not for a million francs

My great and dearest Friend, much time has passed since I've written to you, and I've traveled quite a way since then. I'll say right away that the excursion I was just starting when I sent my last letter has now been completely accomplished (as

Free and Easy

The Way They Loved

"And to love is to travel."
Did they ever get attached to someone, these solitary travelers who never stopped, who claimed they came from nowhere and described themselves as forces in motion? "I learned to run before I could walk," bragged Alexandra David-Néel. "I learned to swim," retorted Anita Conti, "before I could walk." But did they know how to love?

Yes, they did, better than anyone else. Close friendships with other women, plus trust, gratitude, and faithfulness to the men who let them leave—and come back—were the moorings that kept them afloat. Without the love that linked them to cherished beings, adventure would have been unthinkable.

Despite the voyages and the long absences, their feelings were steadfast. It is impossible to overlook the solidity and depth of their relationships: Ella Maillart's friendship with Annemarie Schwarzenbach, the unflagging support she displayed, in Switzerland as well as in Afghanistan, during the direst moments in both their lives; the love, so raw and authentic, between Alexandra and Philippe David-Néel, a steel wire that ran from one to the other, between Asia and Europe, unbroken for forty years; Alexandra's affection for Aphur Yongden, a fourteen-year-old Tibetan boy who abandoned his own family, renounced his inheritance, and left everything behind to follow the Western woman. What did Alexandra love about Yongden, and Yongden about Alexandra? Their shared *spirit of adventure,* of course.

But how did they feel about the ones they left behind, the husbands and lovers who stayed put and awaited their return? Did trailblazing women feel sorrow on leaving them in order to travel the world? Did they feel any regret or nostalgia on departure? Did absence make their hearts grow fonder? Did they feel intense passion once reunited?

In short, trailblazers during this period may have been sincere and loyal friends, but were they also great lovers?

"You want someone at home who is ready to 'hold hands,' 'kiss,' and 'all the rest,'" wrote David-Néel to her husband. "Now that distance has brought a temporary halt to my cooperation, you make me clearly realize that what you liked about me was not me, but the feelings you got from me."

This sweeping assessment was hardly conducive to slipping between the sheets with a partner. And yet even if David-Néel was herself no longer interested in "holding hands and kissing," other, less chaste explorers such as Freya Stark, Rosita Forbes, Margaret Mead, and Emily Hahn, were enthusiastic about "all the rest."

Loving freely—free of hypocrisy and social constraints whatever the nationality, age, or gender of the object of their affection—became the new modus vivendi for adventurous women once the war of 1914–18 had shattered conservative ideals.

Passion had already pushed Fanny Stevenson to flout convention, dropping everything and risking all for the love of a young man nine years her junior. True enough, Robert Louis would become a famous writer. But at the time Fanny went through a divorce for him, the lad showed little promise—he was known to be tubercular, nearly destitute, and dying.

Margaret Mead would follow Fanny Stevenson to the Samoan Islands, and then follow the example of the sexual freedom of young women in the archipelago—the subject of her research. Falling in love with the ethnologists she worked with, Margaret would always find something to suit her *in the field,* and would marry three times.

As for Emily Hahn, her love for a Chinese poet led her to play the role of a concubine in Shanghai's prostitute district for six years. And when she left her poet as World War II broke out, she left him for the head of the British intelligence service, clearly demonstrating how hard it is to shake off adventure.

Since they always navigate on the edge, are adventurous women really able to fulfill the needs of others? Absorbed by their instincts and their quest for absolutes, are they able to listen to the desires

"They never did but what they wanted to
—and their hearts were pure"

of people unlike themselves? Particularly if it means no longer listening to their own voices, perhaps losing their own way?

"People said I bullied Marion," wrote Odette du Puigaudeau, who dragged her companion into the Mauritanian desert, "that I overwhelmed her with my stronger, more enterprising personality. But without my authority, Marion would have remained a secretary at *Eve* despite her diploma and her first prize from the school of fine arts in Rennes. She needed two years in the Sahara in order to find herself again."

So perhaps trailblazing women are revealers, unveilers, and initiators—indeed are facilitators who, like Socrates, encourage other people to "know themselves."

Du Puigaudeau went so far as to change the name of the woman she loved. "You can well imagine that I couldn't write her into my books with such a moniker: Marcelle Borne Kreutzberger!" So "Marcelle" was rechristened "Marion Sénones," a rebirth that delighted both parties. And they went even further. Conforming to the customs of desert Moors, Odette would even pass off Marion as her slave. They were allegedly two chameleons who could adapt, who were gifted at mimicry. Flexible, perhaps; but interchangeable, no. One paved the way, the other followed. They both accepted this casting of roles with confidence and cheerfulness.

Their all-pervading power relationship can be sensed in Odette's comments of despair after Marion's death. "It was my great luck to meet that girl," said du Puigaudeau. "She was the ideal companion, who helped me without getting in the way. She provided my serenity, my moral strength. When she left me, I was like one of those feeble, floppy plants that fall to the ground when you remove its support stake. I was ready to be trampled."

Apparently most of the trailblazing women of the interwar period were able to find harmony only by remaining masters of their souls and their fates. Independent? Egocentric? Competitive? No doubt about it.

As explorers and trailblazers, they galloped ahead. That's all there was to it. The days were long gone when Florence Baker and Jane Dieulafoy *assisted* their husbands. Henceforth women would be the driving force—others would follow behind. But their self-affirmation did not prevent them from admiring, respecting, and even loving the people they led or domineered.

But what happened when a pioneering woman met her twin, her alter ego? Someone as stubborn, as determined, as willing, and as totally free as she?

"Denys and I, whenever we were together, had great luck with lions," wrote Karen Blixen when describing the love of her life. "The early morning air of the African highlands is of such a tangible coldness and freshness that time after time the same fancy there comes back to you: you are not on earth but in dark deep waters, going ahead along the bottom of the sea. It is not even certain that you are moving at all." For a woman who constantly moved forward, who followed her own path despite bankruptcy, illness, and death, the very idea of "not moving" raised questions. She answered such questions with words that perhaps sum up the dream of all the errant women who drop their bags to settle for a moment, an hour, a month, forever: Denys Finch Hatton was always happy to be at her farm because he only went there when the spirit moved him: "He never did but what he wanted to do."

By describing the incarnation of her ideal of love as Freedom—total, absolute, completely uncompromising freedom—Blixen was drawing her own portrait, and that of most pioneering women: *they never did but what they wanted to*—and their hearts were pure.

"Being a woman was no longer a handicap"

Christel Mouchard

A Scent of Liberty

The scent of scandal vanished for good. Being a woman was no longer a handicap when it came to exploring the world, and certain publishers even claimed that it could be an advantage when it came to recounting one's memoirs. Of course there were still people who warned women before they set out, but it was usually only an artifice designed to underscore the dangers (dangers often unavowed by nineteenth-century explorers for fear of hearing the words, "I told you so"). The popularity of accounts by women travelers, however, was not due solely to a certain voyeurism, but also to an appreciation of a feminine viewpoint, a sensibility that colors their photos and their tales, not to mention their humor (the heritage of Mary Kingsley and other damsels full of courage and composure).

Their image became more relaxed. They willingly appeared in jodhpurs and bush jackets, even if they claimed they always kept a nail file and a compact handy. Their audacity was quieter. They began to forget the virtuous strictness required of their elders. Less vigilant, they were easy prey for romance, allowing themselves to be attracted by some appealing men—who didn't necessarily marry them—and allowing themselves to attract some appealing women now and then. This generation of women felt that loving should be just like traveling—free and easy.

When Freya Stark arrived in Baghdad in 1929, Gertrude Bell had been dead for three years. People who had known that great lady of the desert looked with a skeptical eye upon this new Englishwoman who claimed to be an explorer. She had nothing of the elegance that marked Miss Bell's every word and gesture.

Freya Stark
The Happy Wanderer

The newcomer was short and somewhat plump, which did not prevent her from attending diplomatic parties wearing Arab dress, or at least what she thought was Arab dress, her forehead half-masked by a large band designed to hide a large scar that resulted from a youthful accident.

For this unknown, thirty-six-year-old woman, picking up her predecessor's torch would be a difficult task. And yet she would succeed magnificently, to the point of earning the title, some fifty years later, of "the quintessential explorer."

Stark was born in France to an English couple who were keen travelers. She long hesitated over which path to take in life, but a broken engagement, difficult family relationships, an interest in unconventional academic subjects, and the luck of a small annual income steadily drew her to foreign lands. In 1927 she discovered a passion for the Arabic language, and spent several months in Lebanon and Syria. It was a crucial voyage, because from that point onward she decided to make travel an end in itself.

In those days, it was no longer possible to earn the title of explorer simply by moving from one point on the globe to another. Almost everything had already been discovered, and the planet was being crisscrossed by globe trotters of every stripe. You had to find a destination or blank spot on the map where a visit would earn the label of "a world first." Thorough study of the Middle East led Stark to Baghdad, with the intention of reaching the Valleys of the Assassins, a legendary spot where the famous Assassin sect had spread terror in the past. Located in Persia, the valley had not yet been properly mapped. And since Bell had traveled with three mules, two tents, and two servants, Stark decided to go one better

and travel alone, with little or no baggage. Her choice wasn't purely strategic, however—Stark didn't have the funds to mount a true expedition in any case.

On her return to Baghdad in the autumn of 1931, the English community had to admit that a worthy successor to Miss Bell had been found. Not only did Stark reach her goal and return with remarkable scholarly material, but she did so in difficult conditions that revealed the eccentric newcomer's extraordinary stamina. Traveling with minimal baggage and a single guide, exhausted by dysentery and malaria, she nevertheless managed to discover an unknown fortress and to scale an allegedly insurmountable escarpment (in stockings, since her shoes were unsuited to climbing). This expedition was followed by another one, yielding enough material for her first book, *The Valleys of the Assassins,* which earned her not only the respect of specialists in the field but also the honors of the Royal Geographical Society and Royal Asiatic Society.

Two new expeditions in 1935 and 1938, to Hadhramaut, confirmed Stark's calling and her chosen identity, which she cultivated skillfully and effectively. Her droll silhouette and her bold dresses—either by famous French designers, if possible, or else personal concoctions of Oriental garb—won her some unlikely affection from several quarters, especially military men. Witty, talkative, stubborn, sure of herself and others (able to smuggle art on occasion and abandon her scruples when pushed), Stark also managed to earn lasting hostility, especially from her female colleagues.

Her courage and determination, combined with her thorough knowledge of the Arab world, attracted the attention of the British secret services as soon as World War II broke out. Her eccentricity and her friendly, harmless demeanor were weapons she wielded brilliantly in her dealings with Arab political leaders in Egypt, Iraq, Syria, and Palestine.

In her activity as a traveler, Stark appeared to be very much part of her century, a century of ethnographic and spiritual quests; yet in her work as an agent during the war, she appeared to be faithful to her Victorian roots—and perhaps she could be considered the last of the Victorian travelers. Her vision of the Arab world, as admiring as it may have been, remained colored by her love of the British Empire and its values. Although she worked selflessly during the four years of war, her efforts were aimed above all at winning intellectuals to the British cause, in regions already aroused by the anti-colonial ferment. Her

Pages 166 and 167: Freya Stark on a camel; and in Oriental headdress.

Facing page: Freya aged twenty; girls in festive dress in the former protectorate of Aden (now Yemen), 1938.

Above: Freya on the shores of the Tigris, not far from Baghdad.

Above: Mukalla on the coast of Aden,
seen from the heights, in 1935.

Facing page: Ali ibn al-Mansur, sultan
of Seiyun (South Arabia), in the hinterland
of Hadhramaut, 1935; Freya Stark
in her hammock in 1965.

finest achievement, she would later claim, was the founding and running of the Brothers and Sisters of Freedom, a more or less secret organization designed to support the British Crown, whose members were English, Egyptian, Iraqi, and Indian civilians.

The end of the war left this woman of action somewhat at a loose end, as had happened to Gertrude Bell before her. Perhaps that is why she finally found the time to get married. But it didn't last: disappointment was inevitable for a fifty-year-old woman accustomed to unbridled freedom. Stark therefore ended her life as she had led it prior to marriage, alone but surrounded by admirers whom she fascinated and exasperated. Impulsive, a spendthrift, she was always ready to hop from one end of the Middle East to the other, for the fun of it or from financial need, usually both. Thus when over sixty, she decided to follow in the footsteps of Alexander the Great to visit the far reaches of Anatolia, an expedition she completed on her own after abandoning her sole, young traveling companion, a young man initially full of admiration. "I left [him]," she wrote to her publisher, "with that wonderful feeling of exhilaration which seems to visit me when I drop a man." Her lifestyle, which might appear rather haphazard, at any rate brought her remarkable longevity, because she had entered her one hundredth year when she died in 1993. "The true wanderer," she wrote at age seventy-five, "whose travels are happiness, goes out not to shun, but to seek."

She does look very foreign

I look at her in astonishment, for she has so improved with years. She is *much* better looking. She is a little stouter and somehow it suits her, but she has such an air of assurance, a woman of the world accustomed to being made much of, *and* she looks so much happier. . . . There is not a line on her face. She does look very foreign, but of course she is. . . . The last garment I asked about was made in Delhi. . . . Her jewels, lots of them, were very foreign and her coat was a goatskin from Cyprus.

Excerpt from a letter from Mrs. Granville to Lady Lawrence, two friends of the Stark family, written in 1945, when Stark was aged fifty-two. Quoted in Caroline Moorehead, *Freya Stark* (Harmondsworth: Penguin, 1986).

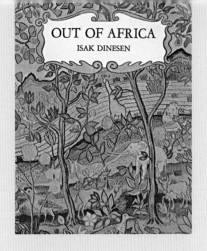

OUT OF AFRICA
ISAK DINESEN

"*I* had a farm in Africa, at the foot of the Ngong Hills." Nostalgia for a vanished world, for an adventure that is over, already in the past: such is the opening sentence of Karen Blixen's *Out of Africa*. But what made Baroness Blixen's farm an "adventure"? Why didn't neighboring plantations give off the same heady fragrance of an exotic, enchanting, and ephemeral paradise?

Karen Blixen

A Tale of Africa

Because they lacked the soul its owner put into her own estate, they lacked a special grave nearby, and above all because they lacked the talent with which she wrote her story. "Told" her story is more like it, because Isak Dinesen—as Baroness Blixen signed her books—was above all a teller of tales.

Born in Denmark in 1885, Karen Dinesen was a demanding young woman who dreaded not living up to her own ambitions. Perhaps that is why she accepted a marriage that lacked love but brought the title of baroness to someone who had been merely a well-educated, upper-middle-class girl from Copenhagen. Probably it was also why she left for Africa, a new land where she could build her own fief far from the constraining fences of well-bred Danish society. Marriage and Africa converged, for that matter: she sailed in January 1914 to join her fiancé, whom she married in Nairobi on arriving in Kenya.

The young Karen realized that her decision was a good one right from her very first day on the African farm. Here she would be queen in her realm. The land was nevertheless harsh, and poorly suited to coffee crops, the price of which was very unstable. But there were the Africans themselves, there was the savanna, there were the lions. She found the Africans unpredictable yet dignified, and as curious about her as she was about them—an opinion far from the conventional one held by most colonists. The savanna and lions meant the excitement of the hunt, camping in the wilderness, and landscapes that evoked the dawn of time.

Other difficulties arose, however, ones that the baroness had not anticipated. They began with her husband, Bror von Blixen, who

conferred syphilis and solitude upon her along with his noble title. Both would accompany Karen throughout her life, to the extent that she would turn them into allies despite the suffering they caused her. "And as for my long sickness," she would write in old age, "do I not owe it indescribably more than I owe to my health?"

Blixen soon realized that her husband decided to live in Africa not so much to become a colonist as to indulge in safaris and affairs of all kinds. She thus often found herself alone on the "farm"—in fact, a plantation of some ten thousand acres bought with funds invested by the Dinesen family. The outbreak of war would increase her attitude of haughty solitude—Bror enlisted in the British army and headed south to the border that separated Kenya from German Tanganyika. In addition to the vagaries of the weather, Karen had to deal with the collapse of commodity prices due to the war, plus the suspicions of English colonists who found her too Danish (and there-fore liable to pro-German sympathies). Yet her isolation was not just imposed, it was also deliberate. Baroness Blixen welcomed a select group that would become and remain her faithful friends, whether adventurers as elusive as Bror (with whom, in spite of everything, she would maintain a very complicated but real friendship) or eccen-tric and somewhat dandyish scholars, all of whom were as crazy about Africa as she was.

Between lion hunting, horse riding, and sophisticated conversa-tion over a bottle of champagne on the veranda, it was a kind of Mount Olympus—rather than paradise—that arose around this

brilliant woman. The gods on this Olympus were almost all hunters who came to live in this part of Kenya to enjoy unbridled pleasure in killing the wild beasts who, they felt, were their peers in strength and cruelty.

The most handsome of these gods was Denys Finch Hatton. He was a legend even among the community of aristocratic adventurers, if less ethereal than Blixen suggested in her autobiographical tale. This son of an earl had no scruples about speculating on African land or lending money at usurious rates if the occasion presented itself. And yet his originality, physical courage, and charm more than made up for his character flaws. His friends saw him as a beloved tyrant, Baroness Blixen viewed him as her ideal incarnate.

They met on April 5, 1918. Both recognized each other as equals, as superior beings who could not be satisfied with an ordinary relationship. The love pact they made implied that one would never be able to possess the other: "An affair of perfect harmony. . . . a deep, burning mutual desire and reverence between two truthful and undaunted creatures, on the same wavelength." Blixen wrote that sentence on the subject of a lion hunt but it might also apply to her relationship to Denys. Respect for the pact would make their affair long and happy, if intermittent. It also meant that Karen Blixen would remain solitary in her world, on her farm.

After the war ended, the world she had created was permanently organized around herself, for she was devoted to making it work. She was the mother and regent of her clan of *totos* (Swahili for

Pages 172 and 173: The front cover of *Out of Africa*; a photo of Karen Blixen on safari.

Facing page: Blixen on a safari in Kenya, 1914; the novelist with her pet owl, 1923.

Above: Fisherman in Kisumu, Kenya, in the early twentieth century.

children): she decided for them, raised, taught, admonished, married, and healed them. She took in sick natives, she housed lost animals, she started a school—all according to her own whim. She transformed her home into an enchanted dwelling thanks to carpets, crystal, sophisticated cuisine, and fragrant flowers. Blixen's African farm was a strange blend of pioneer life and aristocratic refinement, of danger and the good life. It was also a temple erected to Denys Finch Hatton, even if the owner didn't openly admit it, given her pact with him. Everything revolved around the hunter's comings and goings. The dinners she contrived like theater plays were an amorous

TAGET LIGE INDEN MIN
AFREISE TIL AFRIKA.

ceremony during which she would tell her itinerant lover incredibly complicated stories, as though hoping to keep him there a little longer, like some Scheherazade in an evening gown. She sometimes committed to paper her tales, inspired by Nordic sagas and romantic fictions, but she had little confidence in her writing talent; during the sixteen years of her African adventure, her farm was her sole great work, the one into which she put all her strength.

She only became a great writer once Olympus crumbled. By early 1931 the farm was bankrupt. It had to be liquidated, sold at auction. In May of that year Hatton was killed in a plane accident. Africa no longer held anything for Blixen, nothing to which she could devote what little strength her illness left her, no one to whom she could tell her stories.

So she left Africa. And she began writing. In 1934 she published *Seven Gothic Tales,* followed in 1937 by *Out of Africa* and in 1942 by *Winter's Tales.* On two occasions she nearly won the Nobel Prize for Literature, losing first to Ernest Hemingway, then to Albert Camus. She died in 1962 of complications from an anorexia that probably stemmed from her syphilis, from which she never completely recovered. Denys Finch Hatton, meanwhile, stayed in Africa: his remains were buried in the Ngong Hills, on a spot he himself had pointed out once when he and Karen were riding nearby. Long after his death, it was said that lions liked to come and lie at his grave.

Facing page: Baroness Blixen and her servants on the farm in Kenya, 1914.

Above: A portrait of Karen Blixen in 1913; Denys George Finch Hatton.

Above: Blixen posing with her staff in front of her house; her necklace of amber beads was a gift from Farah (second row, left).

Facing page: A portrait of Karen Blixen in 1950.

Each kind of African game

Here in the hills there were Buffaloes. I had even, in my very young days—when I could not live till I had killed a specimen of each kind of African game—shot a bull out here. Later on, when I was not so keen to shoot as to watch the wild animals, I had been out to see them again. I had camped in the hills by a spring half way to the top, bringing my servants, tents, and provisions with me, and Farah and I had been up in the dark, ice cold mornings to creep and crawl through bush and long grass, in the hope of catching a glimpse of the herd.

A short flight at sunset

When Denys and I had not much time for long journeys we went out for a short flight over the Ngong Hills, generally about sunset. These hills . . . are perhaps at their loveliest seen from the air, when the ridges, bare towards the four peaks, mount and run side by side with the airplane, or suddenly sink down and flatten out into a small lawn.

The screech of an eagle

In the Ngong Hills there also lived a pair of eagles. Denys in the afternoons used to say, "Let us go and visit the eagles." . . . . Many times we have chased one of these eagles, careening and throwing ourselves on to one wing and then to the other, and I believe that the sharp-sighted bird played with us. Once when we were running side by side, Denys stopped his engine in mid air, and as he did so I heard the eagle screech.

Karen Blixen, *Out of Africa* (New York: Random House, 1952).

*M*iss Cheesman's biography suggests a nice, quiet life—exotic, perhaps, but quiet. She never sought fame or fortune, just the simple satisfaction of collecting happy memories and a treasure trove of countless little things. None of that would have earned her a place in the annals of exploration if Cheesman's "countless little things" didn't have furry legs, hooked claws, steely jaws, and quivering feelers.

Evelyn Cheesman

The Little Critters' Friend

Cheesman loved spiders and earthworms, among other tiny creatures. It was for *them* that she left her native land, for *them* that she headed into the world's most hostile rain forests, for *them* that she lived among the century's last tribe of cannibals.

If London's school of veterinary medicine had been open to women in 1900, young Miss Cheesman might have had a career treating sheep in Devonshire. But she was frustrated in her veterinary ambitions as her teenage years came to close. She had to content herself with a job as zookeeper in the insect house in Regent's Park Zoo. "Content" should be understood in its most positive sense, because Cheesman was happy in her diminutive realm. Nothing delighted her more, in fact, than the sight of a mygale or a phasmid. These quiet pleasures sufficed until 1923, when the organizers of an entomological expedition to the Pacific invited her to join them. Cheesman was then forty-two. She no longer needed a chaperon, she decided. Once she arrived in Tahiti, she announced to her colleagues that she intended to go collecting on her own, with no equipment other than her hammock, her travel bag, and her insect trays. She was obsessed by one idea: she wanted to find the spider that would prove that New Guinea and the western Pacific isles were once the same landmass.

But she mentioned this to no one, and no one could imagine just how far she would go to satisfy her curiosity—above all not her family, who thought she had a weak constitution. As an entomologist without a degree, she spent thirty years scouring the forests of Melanesia during eight expeditions—all carried out alone. "It seems to be taken for granted that to go alone into wild places like New Guinea, and encamp as I have done at a long distance from any civilized

E. v. d. Hellen, Weimar 1904.
Eingeborener von Beliao beim Auswaschen des Sago.
Kaiser-Wilhelms-Land

people, demands courage. Actually it is not so much courage that is called for but endurance. I should place independence first and then endurance, neither of which are virtues but acquired habits. Independence is regarded as an unsociable habit, especially in a woman, and the dictionary defines self-sufficient as haughty, which shows plainly the general trend of opinion."

Endurance was certainly something Cheesman had, for she managed to withstand weeks of stiflingly humid equatorial forests, putting up with the mud, with the scarcity resulting from the difficulty of getting provisions, with malaria, dengue fever, and with the inevitable bites delivered by her beloved little critters. But every now and then she also needed courage, real courage. As when she inadvertently entered the realm of the Nephile, elegant spiders with long black legs whose webs are large and tough enough to catch small birds: "The webs clung to me, drawing sheets [of webs] after them till I was brought up short, unable to advance another step. Folds within folds clung to my shoulders and arms, and when I stepped backward into what had been a space a moment before, my head came against a very large sheet which enveloped my face like an eastern veil. . . . As for breaking the web, all my force resulted only in cutting my fingers. . . . I even tried to bite the threads but that was useless. All around hung spiders of all ages, some near my face. I did not think them handsome anymore."

It was thanks to a nail file—being a woman can have its advantages—that Cheesman managed to escape this predicament, which

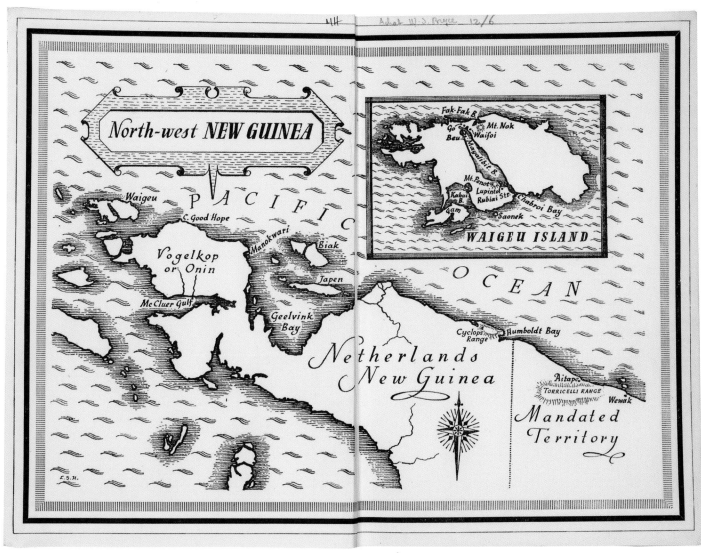

North-west NEW GUINEA

WAIGEU ISLAND

she claimed was far from the worst. "In that wild country there is no danger from carnivorous mammals, there are no lions, tigers, bears, or wolves. Only in the sea are lurking monsters of the deep, only in certain rivers are the voracious little fish which can tear one to pieces; but in rivers, lakes and swamps, and occasionally on an idyllic peaceful seashore, one must beware of the slimy crocodile. Crocodiles and leeches were the only creatures which could horrify me in New Guinea." All that for a love of entomology!

The sole beneficiary of Cheesman's treasure would be London's Natural History Museum, to which she kindly donated each of her harvests, totaling several thousand insects in all. All her expeditions were self-financed—another sign of her spirit of independence—thanks to the royalties on her adventure books (especially *Camping Adventures in New Guinea* and *Time Well Spent*[1]). The museum missed out on just one batch, when a British officer in Papua New Guinea, to whom Cheesman had entrusted specimens gathered during a six-month expedition, allowed them to rot in the tropical rain that flooded the barracks yard. Unembittered, the traveler willingly shared with the army her knowledge of the Melanesian Islands during the war. Evelyn Cheesman died in 1969, aged eighty-eight, a discreet but highly efficient exploring ant.

Pages 180 and 181: The front cover of *Time Well Spent*; and a portrait of Evelyn Cheesman in New Guinea.

Facing page: Postcards from New Guinea.

Above: A map of northwest New Guinea.

Above: Cheesman's notebooks, containing sketches
and observations on her South Sea expeditions;
Cheesman taking makeshift shelter from
the constant tropical rains.

Facing page: Cheesman in New Guinea
with her entomologist's equipment.

A camp in New Guinea

When clear, this slope was so slippery that when we stepped off the platform of the hut we were liable to slide the whole way down until we clutched trees above the precipice. So a fencing of creepers had to be made at the boundaries to avoid broken limbs. That was not a pleasant camp, but from it I worked swamp country below and by contrast it was a relief to get away from liquid mud to the more solid mud of that camp. During the war that locality was occupied by Japanese and I often visualized, when reading the news, rows of little yellow men losing their footing and sliding down that slope into the scrub.

Evelyn Cheesman, *Time Well Spent*
(London: The Travel Book Club, 1960),

*R*osita Forbes was certainly one of the few female explorers to get tangled in a dispute over credit for an exploit with a male counterpart. This sad controversy set her against her desert traveling companion, Ahmed Hassanein Bey, a young Egyptian aged twenty-one. An aristocrat on good terms with the sultan, a graduate of Oxford, and an Olympic medal-winning fencer, Hassanein was mad about history and geography. And he loved his country: in the year 1920 he dreamed of seeing Egypt freed from British domination.

Rosita Forbes

Quarrel at Kufra

The independence movement spurred its leaders to gain a better knowledge of the deserts that made up most of Egypt's territory, whose exploration up till then had too often been left to European curiosity. That was when Hassanein met the young woman whose dreams converged with his, if from a very different path.

Forbes acquired a taste for travel during the war. Born into a Victorian family in 1890, married to a colonel in the British army, she might never have discovered the thrill of danger if she hadn't be encouraged to become a nurse, like many other upper-class women. She was found to have rare skill at the wheel of a vehicle, and became an ambulance driver close to the front. She displayed so much courage under fire that she won two medals—and a divorce from a husband she found too timid.

Once the war was over, she traveled to Australia, India, and the Middle East. On arriving in Cairo, her medals and her background gave her an entrée to the most cultivated circles of the Egyptian administration. There she spoke to Hassanein about the shock of her first experience of the desert, and the ambitions it had stirred in her. The young Egyptian then confided to her a plan he was still keeping secret: to go to Kufra.

The Saharan oasis of Kufra (or Kufara), deep in the middle of the great Libyan desert, had been inaccessible ever since a Muslim sect had made it their capital in the early nineteenth century. The sect's founder, Sidi Muhammed ibn Ali al-Senussi, founded a doctrine, based on Sufism, that spread to a broad part of the central Sahara. The Senussi practiced a particularly strict form of Islam and willingly attacked infidels—in 1879, the German explorer Gerhard Rohlfs barely escaped death when he tried to enter Kufra, and it was

Senussi instigation that was behind the murder of French missionary Charles de Foucauld in 1916. Ever since then, that area of the Sahara had been off-limits to outsiders, whether Christian or Muslim.

Why would an Egyptian aristocrat agree to mount such a dangerous expedition in conjunction with a young Englishwoman who barely spoke Arabic (and who was not, apparently, his lover)? The answer is probably to be found in international politics of the day. The presence of a subject of the world's leading colonial power could constitute an asset in certain diplomatic and financial circumstances; and in all other circumstances, it was easy for a woman to hide beneath a veil, which even an experienced male explorer would have difficulty doing.

That is why Hassanein took the precaution of seeking authorization from Idris al-Senussi (who would become, after World War II, the first and last king of independent Libya, until overthrown by Colonel Gadhafi). But Idris al-Senussi held only limited power over the nomads in his domain, and his decision was immediately challenged by other sheikhs of the sect who, moreover, objected to a white woman accompanying the expedition. Forbes knew what was behind the surprising authorization she had been granted by Idris. "They [the Senussi] liked Hassanein Bey, but they admired and believed in Britain. They wanted us to secure them from Italy. If a British alliance was impossible, they hoped for an Egyptian one."

Placed under such cloudy political auspices, the expedition turned out to be as stormy as feared. Forbes prepared for the trip by

learning Arabic and the female customs of the region, so that she could travel with the purportedly merchant caravan as "Khadija," Hassanein's wife of Circassian origin (a detail that would explain the color of her skin and her poor grasp of Arabic). They endured sand storms, vanished trails, the sight of looters high on surrounding dunes, watering holes that had dried up, tormenting thirst and, worst of all, the suspicions of the nomads they encountered. The Englishwoman nevertheless found the courage to photograph things secretly, from beneath her veil. Once beyond the oasis of Ajdabiya the caravan got lost, the camels fell ill; then it crossed a region of deep ravines and entered a desert of endless white sand. On January 2, Forbes and Hassanein found the human and animal bones of a caravan that had passed that way earlier.

Entering Kufra was no easy task: as soon as the chief of the holy city learned of their presence, the outsiders were thrust into the midst of a terrific quarrel that deepened from hour to hour, some locals accepting the authorization given by Idris, others believing it a forgery and a prelude to invasion. Fortunately for the travelers, the first party won the argument, and Forbes could thus claim to be the first Westerner to have entered the "forbidden oasis."

The real polemic broke out once the partners returned to their respective nations. On the one hand Forbes was accused of minimizing the role played by Hassanein, while on the other hand a columnist in the Cairo daily *Al-Ahram* claimed on Hassanein's behalf that, "after returning, he confessed that he had made certain mistakes that he intended to avoid the second time around. Above all, he had

Pages 186 and 187: Forbes posing on a horse; a portrait of Rosita Forbes.

Facing page: Forbes dismounting from a camel; Forbes pausing for refreshment.

Above: Forbes in Oriental dress, November 1926.

Above and facing page: Forbes in Bedouin dress; and on a camel.

agreed to allow a certain British woman, Mrs. Rosita Forbes, to accompany him into the desert. Forbes pleaded with him to let her replace another British person who had been unable to join the expedition, and Hassanein, reputedly the consummate gentleman, agreed." On closer inspection, it would seem that the alleged positions of both protagonists were more the work of journalists than the travelers themselves, who in their own texts show much more respect for each other than later interpretations would suggest.[1]

So was it the Forbes expedition or the Hassanein Bey expedition? The subsequent careers of the two companions show that it is impossible to decide. The Egyptian would continue the systematic exploration of his own country, while Forbes, in 1924, would be among the first Europeans to cross Abyssinia, an adventure that resulted in a film, *From Red Sea to Blue Nile*. Then she led an expedition in search of the last isolated Indians in the Panamanian jungle. In 1928, she drove a car from Peshawar to Samarkand, passing through Kabul, Bamiyan, Mazar-i-Sherif and finally Uzbek Turkistan. Having married another colonel, she ended her days peacefully in the Bahamas in 1965.

People who knew both Hassanein and Forbes noted that, in addition to a taste for travel and adventure, they both shared an insistence on elegance that brooked no exceptions. Whereas the former took bath salts and a dinner jacket on their clandestine expedition, the latter was famous for her hats, one of which a witness would later describe as "the most startling cart-wheel that had ever been seen at Ascot."

Once the voyage was over, Forbes reassumed her English identity

There I discarded my worn
barracan with a sigh of relief,
yet, as I wandered through the
honeycomb of old Siwa, with
its close-piled houses one upon
another and its labyrinth of dark
tunnels that serve as streets,
I was ashamed before the gaze
of Arabs. It seemed to me
intolerable that a Moslem
should see my face unveiled.
Instinctively, I pulled at my hat
brim and my flying cloak, for,
curiously, the soul of this people
had become mine and
I resented the lack of privacy
till I remembered that the Sitt
Khadija was no more!

Rosita Forbes, *The Secret of the Sahara
Kufara* (London: Long Rider's Guild
Press, 2000), 309.

Was Margaret Mead aware
of the constraints her predecessors
had to adopt in order to be earn
acceptance as a geographer, botanist,
or anthropologist? Perhaps not.
With nary a look backward,
she shrugged off corset, skirts,
and social conventions. She was
convinced that being an advocate
of free love would not prevent her
from being accepted as a great
scientist, just as she had
no fear that her tumultuous
personal life would upset any
bigwigs, except perhaps for
some jealous colleagues—one
of whom was a former lover[1].

Margaret Mead

Love of Science, Science of Love

It's a pity you're not a boy, you would have gone far." Mead's father, a professor of economics, must have guessed comments of this type would double the natural energy already displayed by his daughter, then a student at prestigious Barnard College. Being a woman, after all, hadn't prevented the professor's own wife from becoming a sociologist.

Margaret opted for anthropology, encouraged by two teachers: Frank Boas, who was already famous in the field, and Ruth Benedict, who soon became a close—indeed very close—friend (or, to be more specific, a lover to the young student who was as attractive as she was intelligent). It was Boas who assigned Mead her first mission in what became her "field," namely a study of the population of Samoa to see whether the adolescent behavior observed in Western countries had its counterpart in other societies.

Boas hadn't chosen this student at random. Four feet eleven inches tall, youthful in body, with an impish face, Mead could easily have passed for a teenager herself, even though two years earlier she had already married Luther C. Cressman, a pastor and archaeologist.

Boas was right on target. For an eight-month period, from September 1925 to May 1926, the apprentice anthropologist lived among young Samoan girls like a fish in water. Almost invisible, she observed them, listened to their confidences, and shared their secrets and sex lives, noting everything. And she returned with the material for a book that would immediately launch her into the ranks of great anthropologists: *Coming of Age in Samoa* confirmed the hypothesis according to which adolescence was a Western cultural phenomenon rather than a physiological inevitability. The popularity of this

theory was probably partly due to the fact that it converged with an intellectual trend fashionable in New York. Mead made no secret of the fact that she studied foreign cultures in the hope of better understanding her own culture—and also of changing it, though she was less open about that aspect.

Indeed, one question haunted her work: might the ease with which young Samoan women entered adulthood not be related to their sexual freedom, both heterosexual and homosexual? She would be heavily criticized for this ideological presupposition by the academic generation that followed her own; and it is impossible to ignore the fact that Mead's practice and defense of sexual freedom guided her research, that her love life was closely linked to her studies.[2] But what may make her suspect in the eyes of twenty-first century anthropologists makes her absolutely fascinating in the eyes of the historian of social trailblazers.

In 1928, Mead divorced her first husband and immediately married Reo Fortune, a New Zealand anthropologist who was studying the population of the nearby islands of New Guinea (Manus). Mead adopted this region for her second field study, which resulted in a book published in 1930, *Growing Up in New Guinea*. Once again, she compared the way children were brought up in the United States with what she and Fortune observed in the Papuan society in which they lived. And once again, it was not hard to read between Mead's lines: American society should profit from this lesson to consider a sweeping liberation of it own mores.

After receiving her doctorate from Columbia University in 1929, Mead left for a third field study. This time, she and her husband headed for the interior of New Guinea, to the Sepik River region, whose cultural diversity was legendary. They wanted to pursue research into differentiation between male and female roles. And now they intended to benefit from the material and intellectual cooperation of a famous ethnologist, Gregory Bateson, who at that very moment was studying the Iatmul, a Sepik people close to their own subjects. The encounter took place in a region of the world reputed to be one of the most dangerous and inhospitable on the planet due to its equatorial climate and its isolated populations with warlike habits. The three ethnologists were certainly cut off from the rest of the world, while being surrounded by men and women whose mores were alien to their own, to say the least (it was a highly eroticized culture, wrote Mead). They closely observed their subjects' every gesture, especially if it might have sexual connotations. It was a strange atmosphere, complicated not only by bouts of malaria with incumbent hallucinations, but also by the collision of three very strong personalities. The trio formed an uneasy mélange of intellect and sensuality (the latter all the more open in an effort to indicate its acceptance). An affair sprang up between Mead and Bateson right under the eyes of Fortune, who was ultimately less interested in free love than his two companions; a violent scene eventually occurred, complete with blows and insults, ending in a miscarriage for Mead and a hasty departure from New Guinea.

Pages 192 and 193: Mundugumor painting, 1932; Margaret Mead in the Samoan Islands, 1926.

Facing page: Mead and young Samoan women in 1926; in a canoe, two years later, with children from Manus, one of the Admiralty Islands of Papua New Guinea.

Above: Boys from Pere Village, Manus, Admiralty Islands, 1928.

The drama did not hinder publication of another book in 1935, which would become yet another classic of ethnology: *Sex and Temperament in Three Primitive Societies* (a title that might seem droll if taken ironically). That same year Mead divorced Fortune, and the following year she married Bateson.

Their marriage would last fifteen years, the happiest and most serene years of Mead's life. The Batesons left together for Bali on a new field study that would be less focused but more ambitious than their previous work: this time they wanted to gather all available data on Balinese culture, not just in terms of mores but also in terms of dance, painting, and theater. In all, Bateson and Mead would collect fifteen hundred artworks, make a film, and take twenty-five thousand photographs.

The anthropological couple's next subject of study was infinitely more modest: named Catherine, she was born in 1939 and right from her first day provided her mother with a wonderful source of observation, Mead having won recognition as a specialist in comparative educational techniques. This period also saw the publication of *Balinese Character* (1942) and *Growth and Culture* (1951), not to mention the propaganda texts Mead wrote during the war for the Office of War Information.

After the war—and another divorce—Mead firmly and comfortably enjoyed her hard-earned status of intellectual icon. She published and lectured widely on bringing up children. Margaret Mead died of cancer in 1978, after having published her memoirs, *Blackberry Winter,* in 1972.[3]

Facing page: Reo Fortune and Margaret Mead in Pere Village, 1928.

Above: Mead and young flute players in Alitoa, New Guinea, 1932; Mead interviewing people on Bali, 1937 (photo taken by Gregory Bateson).

Above and left: Margaret Mead and Gregory Bateson in Tambunam, 1938; a Samoan couple on Butaritari Atoll in the Kiribati group.

Facing page: Margaret Mead on December 12, 1936.

Benefits of travel

As the traveler who has once been from home is wiser than he who has never left his own doorstep, so a knowledge of one other culture should sharpen our ability to scrutinize more steadily, to appreciate more lovingly, our own.

Margaret Mead, *Coming of Age in Samoa*, 1928

Letter from a concerned professor to a young ethnology student

Dear Margaret,
I suppose the time is drawing near when you want to leave. Let me impress upon you once more first of all that you should not forget your health. I am sure you will be careful in the tropics and try to adjust yourself to conditions and not work when it is too hot and moist in the daytime. If you find that you cannot stand the climate do not be ashamed to come back. There are plenty of other places where you could solve the same problem on which you propose to work.

Letter from Frank Boas to Margaret Mead, July 14, 1925 (manuscript in the Library of Congress, Washington, DC).

"What is the good of sending people round the world? I have done it: it doesn't help. It only kills time. You return just as unsatisfied as you left. Something more has to be done."

Ella Maillart may have been the first woman to raise this issue. Not that nineteenth- century women didn't seek to "do something more," but people didn't express it in the same way. Their "more"— philanthropic commitment or botanical research—was less an individual quest than a way of conforming to social values: a woman might travel, fine, but she should at least be of some service to her country.

Ella Maillart

Far from the Chaos of the West

Maillart was resolutely different from her predecessors. She displayed no patriotism, no ethnocentrism, nor even any rejection of the society from which she came. A product of the anxiety that clouded Europe in the 1930s, she pursued a physical and spiritual quest that belonged solely to her.

Her youth, spent on the shore of Lake Geneva, was golden yet unsatisfying. "Except when I was sailing or skiing I felt lost, only half alive. Everything I saw or read was depressing. The 'war to end war' was bringing in its train compromises, artificial ideals, and palavers that failed to establish a real peace. Growing uneasiness and lack of security seemed to confirm what Spengler had called the 'decline of the West.'"

Spending winters in the mountains, summers on a sailboat, Maillart briefly taught French in an English school but never sought to follow the path that took well brought-up girls where they were supposed to go. Apparently she was not attracted to either marriage or men, and even less attracted to social or professional success. Her parents, who dealt in the fur trade, were moderately worried about their sole daughter's unprofitable passion for the great outdoors. "What are you going to do with your life? Surely you can't turn your life into a nonstop vacation?" Even when her father asked her this question one fine day in 1920, he couldn't imagine the heights to which his daughter would take the art of itinerant idleness.

Maillart wanted to be independent of her times, independent of her milieu. Perhaps it was that very personality trait that made her a true reporter.

In the USSR, for example: the image she provided in her first book, *Parmi la jeunesse russe* (Among Russian Youth), written in 1932

Pages 200 and 201: The walls and palace of the Kremlin, seen from Dom Sovietov (House of Soviets), Moscow, 1930; Ella Maillart reading Paul Valéry, Quinghai Province, China, 1935.

Above: The valley of Bamiyan, Afghanistan, in 1937.

Facing page: A schooner at the edge of Lake Issyk-Kul in Kirgiziya with, in the foreground, a caravan of wool, 1932; Annemarie Schwarzenbach and Ella Maillart leaving Geneva for Kabul in 1939.

following a trip across the Caucasus Mountains in the company of some Russian students, was quasi-ethnographic in its neutrality and accuracy. In those years, however, such a subject was not conducive to cold objectivity; Maillart's neutrality was criticized by her Swiss compatriots, who would have preferred that she take a hard look at the Stalinist regime and its human impact. In all her travels, however, Maillart would retain this aloofness, this ability to observe without judging. She remained naturally, spontaneously calm. Strangely, she didn't like to write, because writing "cannot manage to express the most important things, which remain unfathomable." Indeed, this traveler remained unfathomable herself; she was above all a neutral eye that moved across Asia, an eye that remained steady as long as the body was in movement.

This detachment lent a particular tone to Maillart's most famous expedition, which provided the material for a book that would become a classic of travel writing—quite an accomplishment for a woman who didn't like to write. When Maillart found herself in Peking in 1934, she was already a veteran adventurer: she had sailed yachts with her female friend Miette, then with a crew of four women, and finally alone in the Olympic Games of 1924; she had discovered the pleasure of trekking across the steppes and meeting the people—her trip across the Caucasus had been followed by another, in Turkistan, where she met the Kyrgyz, Kazakh, and Uzbek people. It was during this latter expedition that, scaling a 16,000-foot summit, she glimpsed the Takla-Makan desert, located in the

forbidden region of China. This legendary spot fueled a dream that she swore she would fulfill one day. Alone, she returned west via the southern republics that were torn by the bloody repression of the Soviet army on the Muslim peoples who had risen up. Maillart traveled without a permit and therefore avoided heavily traveled routes and crossroads (a habit she would retain, as though proclaiming her independence). This exploit would be recounted in *Turkistan Solo*, which won her a solid reputation in journalistic circles. And that is why an illustrated periodical, *Le Petit Parisien*, dispatched Maillart to China to report on Manchuria, then under Japanese occupation.

Once in Beijing, however, Maillart was less interested in politics than in wide open spaces, all the more attractive for being off-limits due to four years of civil war. The thought of heading to India via the forbidden territories of Xinjiang and Karakoram intrigued her; defying the ban became all the more appealing once the Swedish explorer Sven Hedin had suggested an unusual way of skirting it. Northern Tibet and Qaidam, he told her, was so difficult to reach that the Chinese government didn't even bother to monitor the borders. Maillart, who could be fairly sociable and easygoing, didn't hesitate to mention her project to English reporter Peter Fleming, whom she had first met in London and encountered again in Beijing. Their conversation, as she later recounted it, summed up the testy friendship that bound this pair of travelers. "As a matter of fact, I'm going back to Europe by that route," stated Fleming on hearing her idea. "You can come with me if you like," but Maillart cut him off:

"I beg your pardon, [but] it's I who'll take you, if I can think of some way in which you might be useful to me."

Their relationship remained a solid one, if delicately poised between competitiveness and humor, becoming a non-violent conflict that lasted seven months and 3,500 miles. Maillart commented on the time she held Fleming from being thrown out of a truck: "I had saved his life, but he complained that I had hurt him."

In February 1935, the two travelers left Peking with travel permits as far as Koko Nor. From there, to avoid military patrols, they headed for the unknown vastness of the high plateau of Qaidam with its icy winds. They reached Xinjiang and headed on to the Pamirs via the Silk Road. Finally they arrived in Srinagar, in Kashmir. Neither of them would say much about the sufferings they endured, preferring to describe the anecdotes, encounters, and breathtaking landscapes that they crossed at the slow but compelling pace of their camels.

On her return to Paris, Maillart was described by Paul Morand as follows: "The woman. . . . is dressed in lambskin boots and gloved in mittens, her skin burnt by mountain air and desert winds, exploring inaccessible regions of the earth in the company of Chinese, Tibetans, Russians and Englishmen whose socks she mends, whose wounds she heals, and with whom she sleeps in all innocence under the stars." As to Fleming, faithful to English understatement, he simply described his companion as full of courage and curiosity;

much later, in a never-published obituary, he commented that she never married. Significantly, each member of the pair would recount their shared journey in two separate books, Maillart in *Forbidden Journey* (1936) and Fleming in *News from Tartary* (1936). With hindsight, it seems miraculous that this expedition, doomed to failure as much by the personalities of its protagonists as by the goal they set themselves, became one of the most famous voyages of the twentieth century.

The very sobriety of her book expressed Maillart's courage much better than any dramatization might have done, and its success enabled her to continue to live from her travels. As a reporter, she wrote for *Le Petit Parisien* until 1939, visiting Turkey, India, Iran, and Afghanistan, traveling by truck and by bus. Then she undertook an adventure that was perhaps the most unusual—certainly the most poignant—of all. *The Cruel Way* was the title of the book in which Maillart recounted a voyage taken in the company of a novelist friend, Annemarie Schwarzenbach. The latter was a sensitive, profoundly anti-Nazi writer who was also homosexual, addicted to morphine, and suicidal, and who felt that genius was inseparable from sorrow. According to Maillart, Schwarzenbach "believed in suffering. She worshipped it as the source of all greatness. And that day for the first time I asked myself if she was able to bear her misery because something in her enjoyed it? If so, would she be able to complete that movement, thus turning hell into heaven?" It was to give Schwarzenbach a chance to transform her own fate that Maillart

Facing page: Blizzard in Boron Kol Valley, Qaidam, China, 1935; caravan pass above Hunza valley, Kashmir, also 1935.

Above: Along the edge of the Kabul River, Afghanistan, October 1939; the giant Buddha of Bamiyan, 175-feet high, in 1939.

Above: Peter Fleming playing cards in Qinghai Province, 1935; a map showing the route from Beijing to India.

suggested they travel together, in a Ford, to Afghanistan via Istanbul, Trebizond, Tehran, and Herat. But Schwarzenbach would not abandon "the cruel way." The more the car bucked over desert trails, the deeper she sank. Soon every stop was an occasion for Schwarzenbach to seek out first a dealer, then a lair in which she could descend ever deeper into a drugged stupor. Maillart no longer knew how to save her friend, she felt her outstretched hand slowly lose its grip. So she sought to consolidate her inner peace, to summon up "the secret of a harmonious life," which she found in the world all around her. "The early morning filled me with delight. The colors were bright but mellow, as if edged with mother-of-pearl. . . . To the north, beyond the pink cliffs and their sculpted figures,[1] rose high hills with velvety blue furrows dotted here and their with little blots of snow."

The two friends returned at the end of 1940, painfully united by a shared sense of failure. Schwarzenbach died two years later in a banal cycling accident, her body exhausted. When a distressed Maillart heard the news, she was far away from war-torn Europe. She was far from the chaos, far from any political or patriotic commitment. She had withdrawn from the clash of weapons and ideas. Her attitude to war was a logical outcome of the options she had adopted

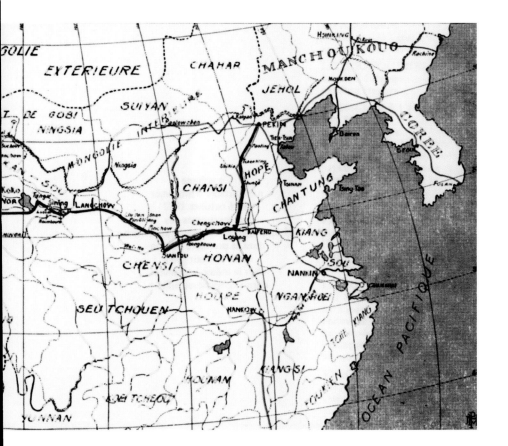

from expedition to expedition. It reveals the extent to which Maillart differed from contemporary fellow travelers such as a Freya Stark, Louise Arner Boyd, and Odette du Puigaudeau, all of whom resembled their predecessors in the way they joined the war effort in the service of their countries. Maillart, in contrast, moved to India. This period of her life was recounted in a manner that deliberately underscored her refusal to act: 'Ti-Puss was the story of her life in India with a pussycat. The animal served as an excuse for Maillart to recount the teachings of two Hindu masters, a silent path that took its mistress far from the material world "because a cat," explained Maillart, "incarnates the fullness of being." After the war, the traveler would remain on the harmonious path she had blazed for herself. On returning to Europe, she organized cultural and spiritual voyages, gave lectures, and moved to Chandolin, a village high in the Swiss mountains, where she remained until her death on January 27, 1997. It was Maillart herself who, without abandoning her usual reserve, provided the best key for understanding her approach. "The journey lengthens, and at times it seems as though it will only end when life ends; you feel like a passive thing carried along powerlessly."

Annemarie: traveling, not deciding

This voyage does not require us to make decisions nor does it put our conscience before a choice that makes us guilty or repentant, humble or stubborn.

From an article by Annemarie Schwarzenbach, published in *National Zeitung* in April 1940, quoted in Oliver Weber, *Je suis de nulle part—sur les traces d'Ella Maillart* (Paris: Payot, 2003).

Ella: why go home?

I should have liked the journey to continue for the rest of my life. There was nothing to attract me back to the west. I knew I should feel isolated amongst my contemporaries, for their ways had ceased to be my ways.

Ella Maillart, *Forbidden Journey from Peking to Kashmir* (London: Marlboro Press, 2003).

Osa among the pygmies, Osa stroking a crocodile, Osa astride a zebra, Osa shooting a lion, Osa in a pilot's uniform—Osa Johnson presented multiple pictures of herself, always different yet always the same, taken in the most exotic settings in the world. While it is sometimes hard to find photographs of early woman travelers—who would have been able to snap Mary Kingsley as she tickled a hippopotamus's ear with the tip of her umbrella?—it is equally difficult to find an episode in Johnson's adventures that is not illustrated by the pretty, impish, delightful Osa.

Osa Johnson

The Power of a Picture

So much so that we might overlook the fact that she was much more than a "pinup" for travel documentaries—she was a true explorer.

When she met her future husband in 1910, Osa Leighty knew what she was getting into. Martin Johnson already had a pronounced taste for adventure. He had been aboard the *Snark,* the sailboat on which Jack London and Charmian Kittredge had crossed the Pacific a few years earlier. Johnson had only stopped in Osa's little hometown in Kansas long enough to give a lecture on his cruise in the tropics. Kansas is flat, monotonous, and a long way from the sea. Sixteen-year-old Osa looked like Dorothy from *The Wizard of Oz.* Like Dorothy, she would fly over the rainbow, leaving Kansas far behind, in the guise of a voyager.

However, even rainbows won't get you anywhere without money. Married at sixteen, Osa followed Martin on his lecture tour. He spoke and she performed songs, in the hopes of garnering enough funds to organize another expedition. By 1917, they were ready. The Johnsons left with a plan to film, for the first time, the famous "Big Nambas" on Malekula Island in the New Hebrides (now Vanuatu). Martin had to be careful; he knew the tribe's reputation for cannibalism was no exaggeration, thanks to firsthand accounts by traders he met in Jack London's company. And indeed, the first contact was disastrous. After having set themselves up comfortably to shoot their first documentary, the naive young couple was taken prisoner by their hosts, who had mimed hospitality the better to lure them inland. Fortunately, the arrival of a ship in the bay convinced the Big Nambas to release the two white,

would-be filmmakers—who still had to race as fast as they could through the tropical forest before their ship weighed anchor.

This little miracle defined their future life. They managed to salvage their footage, and the resulting film, *"Cannibals of the South Seas"*, represented a watershed in the history of the movies. Henceforth the general public could see what had previously been the preserve of intrepid adventurers, ethnographers, and sailors; audiences could now experience fear of Big Nambas without ever leaving their comfortable, red-plush seats. Americans could hardly refuse such fun—the film was a smash hit.

When the Johnsons set off again, they left with a film crew and enough money to transform the next trip into a professional affair. They even enjoyed the luxury of filming the Big Nambas in the act of watching themselves on a silver screen, set up in the heart of forest. Peaceful cannibals were suddenly transformed into Hollywood actors.

After the cannibals came big game. Employing the latest film-making equipment, Osa and Martin pointed their lens at Africa. Once again, what had formerly been the preserve of adventurers could henceforth be experienced by the American public, which delighted in being able to take part in a lion's feast, in the death of a zebra, in elephantine lovemaking. The Johnsons were not scientists, nor even journalists, just good image-hunters and shrewd business-people. They were ready to do whatever necessary to catch sight of a leopard or buffalo. Thus one day, while Martin was

filming a herd of rhinoceroses, he was charged by a large male—but neither he nor Osa fled or tried to dodge. Osa calmly shouldered her rifle and fired. The animal collapsed in front of the filmmaker, who didn't miss a single frame of action. Unsurprisingly, their first animal film, *Trailing African Wild Animals,* was wildly popular. So they soon hit the trail again. In fact, they were constantly organizing expeditions throughout their twenty-seven years of marriage.

As time went by, their fame grew—and so did their expeditions. In the 1930s, an African safari required 235 porters. Osa, no longer a little girl from Kansas, was responsible for the organization, which everyone agreed was flawless. And when the undertaking called for aircraft, she learned to pilot *Osa's Ark* above the savannas. The Johnsons were the first people to fly over Mount Kilimanjaro and Mount Kenya. Unfortunately, the spectacular—indeed, somewhat indulgent—side of their pictures sometimes makes us forget the patience and boldness required to get such

Pages 208 and 209: Teddy, the Johnsons' chimpanzee, learned to imitate them surprisingly quickly; Osa Johnson checks her rifle during a safari in Africa, 1934.

Facing page: Martin Johnson screened his first film on the Big Nambas at Malekula in 1919; a photo of Big Nambas next to large, carved tom-toms decorated with boar tusks, Vao Islands, New Hebrides, 1919.

Above: Martin shooting with his famous Akeley camera in the Meru region of Kenya.

Above, clockwise: Poster for *Trailing African Wild Animals*; the *Spirit of Africa* flying over a herd of elephants in the Lorian swamplands of Kenya in 1933; Osa on a zebra in Kenya; the two anthropologists in Kenya in 1930.

Facing page: Osa Johnson gives a demonstration on how to use makeup, April 30, 1923.

images. When shooting what would be their last film in 1935, on Borneo, they had to spend two full years on the island. They followed the course of rivers on raft and canoe, they were the first to explore the Kinabatangan River, and the first to stay among the Tenggara headhunters—all the while tracking crocodiles and orangutans, eye glued to the camera and hand ready on the crank.

Between 1917 and 1937, Osa and Martin Johnson made eight films, took thousands of still photos, and published nine books. Their adventure came to an end in American skies, when a storm overtook the commercial airplane taking them to yet another lecture. Martin died of his injuries and Osa left the hospital seriously handicapped. She nevertheless continued the lecture tour, in a wheelchair. Only a heart attack in 1953 brought her nomadic lecture career to an end, along with her plans to return to Africa one more time.

First encounter with "cannibal peoples"

Returning look for look with the regal chief, Nagapate, Martin spoke casually to me. "Get on down that trail with the carriers, Osa. I'll follow. Do as I tell you, and hurry."

Nagapate was not to be diverted, however, and caught me as I turned away. He took my hand and shook it just as Martin had shaken his. My relief was so great at what seemingly had turned into a friendly leave-taking that I laughed and heartily returned the shake. This may have been a mistake. At any rate, when I tried to withdraw my hand, he closed his first hard upon it, and then began experimentally to pinch and prod my body. I choked back a scream and looked wildly toward Martin. His face was bloodless, and fixed in a wooden smile.

Osa Johnson, *I Married Adventure: The Life and Adventures of Martin and Osa Johnson* (New York: Willima Morrow, 1940)

Odette was lanky, haughty, brilliant. Marion was short, round, smiling. Odette wrote, Marion painted. They were lovers.

Back in that month of 1934, they set out together to cross the deserts of Mauritania on camelback. The figure they cut together in that landscape of sand and nomadic tents was so uncommon—strange, even—that Moors would call 1934 "the year of the two ladies."

Odette du Puigaudeau

The Year of the Two Ladies

The two ladies had been living together for over a year. Odette du Puigaudeau was an aristocrat from Brittany, the daughter of the artist Ferdinand du Puigaudeau, related to Alphonse de Chateaubriand. Raised in a ruined manor by a father who taught her to draw, and a strict mother who served as her schoolteacher, Odette had a solitary childhood full of boredom and dreams. In 1920 she left for Paris, where she earned a living as a draftsman for the Musée d'Histoire Naturelle, then as an assistant designer for Lanvin. When she met Marion Sénones, she had also made a minor name for herself as a journalist who specialized in subjects related to Brittany.

Marion's real name was Marcelle Borne Kreutzberger. She was the daughter of a French civil servant from Auxerre. Her mother allowed her to enroll in the school of fine arts, which was most unusual for a sixteen-year-old girl in 1902. For a long time Marion lived with Madeleine Anglada, a wealthy, unconventional pediatrician. She was an editorial secretary for the magazine *Eve* when, in 1932, Odette du Puigaudeau came to the office in search of assignments.

"A special rapport sprang up between us," confided du Puigaudeau to her biographer.' This rapport carried them to the coasts of Africa. Du Puigaudeau was always in front, having been determined for a number of years to undertake some uncommon adventure; Sénones followed behind, silent but even sturdier than her friend. Their goal was to gather archaeological material that would document the life that had flourished in the Sahara during the neolithic era. In order to fulfill that goal, they had been in touch with Théodore Monod, an expert who indicated the specific zones where searches might prove fruitful.

On January 12, 1934, they mounted camels for the first time at Memghar, and set out on the trail to Nouakchott, guarded by four Moorish warriors. They were traveling dressed in jellabas and the baggy trousers called *serwal*, they slept on the ground, and they ate little—yet their bags contained a compact and lipstick, just in case. After two difficult weeks acquiring the habit of riding camels, they started to become true nomads. Du Puigaudeau discovered that her aristocratic education had been a wonderful preparation for living among the Moors. So wonderful, in fact, that she naturally wound up not lifting a finger in the caravan, all manual labor being considered unworthy of a master by her hosts in those days. We don't know how this perfect acculturation sat with gentle Marion, who was presented as du Puigaudeau's "slave" on behalf of the cause. Since she took up her pencils when du Puigaudeau took up her pen,

Sénones left no record of her impressions apart from her drawings—she remains the mystery of this grand adventure.

After a few more weeks, however, the two Frenchwomen discovered the limits of Moorish "friendship." Once past Aleg, on the edge of Trab el-Bidan, they left the regions protected by French colonial outposts. Hence they were totally in the hands of the "lords" with whom du Puigaudeau had gotten on so well—but who now became as contemptuous as they had earlier been respectful. "The revenge of our disgrace," wrote du Puigaudeau without bitterness, "was that, in the end, the real masters were the camels." The situation worsened when the little caravan reached the edge of Black Africa, a swampy region where the camels had difficulty advancing through the crazed mud. A fall left Sénones with a persistent pain in her head, while du Puigaudeau succumbed to a fever that resulted from a poorly treated infection on her finger. Finally, despite a halt of three weeks in Kiffa, the two women had to be evacuated in all haste to Dakar, where du Puigaudeau had her finger amputated.

But they did not give up. In July they headed north, first in a truck and then in an army vehicle, accompanied by French infantry troops—the Adrar gorges where they were traveling were the site of frequent ambushes by looters. The two women carried on to Chinguetti, nicknamed "the Sorbonne of the Desert" in honor of the Koranic manuscripts carefully preserved there; then they headed for Ouadane. All along the route, they recorded rock engravings and

Pages 214 and 215: Odette du Puigaudeau and Marion Sénones in Mauritania; a photo of du Puigaudeau on a camel.

Facing page, counterclockwise: Du Puigaudeau and Sénones in their cabin on *La Belle Hirondelle*, a lobster ship sailing for Mauritania, November 30, 1933; the two women with their pet leopard in the offices of *Le Petit Parisien*, February 17, 1938, after returning from Mauritania; dressed as a man going by the name of Marcel Dupuis, du Puigaudeau carried out an investigative report on the Paris stock market in 1935.

Above: At the home of the chief of the Laghals in Chinguetti, Mauritania, 1937.

Above: Setting up a real camp; the two women posing in a studio in Paris.

paintings, discovered an ossuary, and gathered all traces of prehistoric Saharan life, such as arrowheads, stone beads, ostrich eggs, and so on.

On August 15, it was time to head back to the coast—another three hundred miles on camelback. "I was fed up with Moorish tea," admitted du Puigaudeau, "and had had my fill of campfires, sand, sandstorms, and the sight of sand!" They returned to Paris after having traveled fifteen hundred miles on camel and twelve hundred miles by car, rich with hundreds of photographs and an enormous amount of archaeological material that they donated to the Musée Ethnographique.

We can only assume that they felt a certain nostalgia for sand and campfires after all, because they soon headed back to the Sahara, this time to Timbuktu, where they joined the *azalai,* an annual caravan of several thousand camels that crossed the northern, most arid region of the desert to the salt mines in the Taoudeni basin. Once again, their voyage ended with success.

The war brought the two ladies' wanderings to a halt. For several years they founded and ran an association to aid French prisoners of war in Germany. But they hit the trail one more time, between 1949 and 1951; having become specialists on Mauritania, they subsequently gave numerous lectures and published many articles until Sénones died in 1977. Du Puigaudeau lived on until 1991 in Morocco, driven from her beloved lands by decolonization. Fortunately, a curator at France's Bibliothèque Nationale, Monique Vérité, tracked her down in Rabat prior to her death, in order to record her final recollections of her superb story of love and desert life.[2]

Everything to learn

I came, barefoot and empty-handed,
with the desire to make contact and
establish friendship. I had to learn
everything from the Moors, and they
influenced me more than I influenced
them.

Quoted by Monique Vérité in *Odette du
Puigaudeau, une Bretonne au désert*
(Paris: Éditions Jean Picollec, 1992).

Desert silences

We steadily drove deeper and
deeper into the silence. A silence
that was not a halt, a pause,
or a passage, but a permanent,
fundamental order, the sum
of multiple silences established
in large concentric circles, from
horizon to horizon, across
an empty vastness.

Odette du Puigaudeau, "Léçons du Sahara"
(unpublished manuscript), quoted by
Monique Vérité in *Odette du Puigaudeau,
une Bretonne au désert*
(Paris: Éditions Jean Picollec, 1992).

Eyes scanning the distant
horizon, skin weathered by salty
air, Anita Conti could have
been a hero straight
out of a Hemingway novel,
embarked on an endless quest
to land some huge fish—a cod
off Newfoundland, a shark
off Senegal, or a sawfish
off some other coast.
Conti was less interested
in sailing the oceans than
in exploring and exploiting
them (in the best sense
of the word).

Anita Conti

The Young Woman and the Sea

The feeling that took her to sea was not so much fascination or enchantment—concepts associated with legendary sailors—as a sense of personal belonging. Indeed, Conti was practically born in the sea. Her parents dipped her in the ocean just a few days after her birth—"I could swim before I could walk," she used to say. The reasons behind this precocious swim in the ocean were more than merely poetic. Her father, Leven Caracotchian, a wealthy surgeon of Turkish-Armenian stock, was a fan of hygienics, a school of medicine that advocated good health through sports and outdoor activities. Conti thus grew up in a world where the sea was considered not just a fine subject for a painting or a huge swimming pool for vacationers, but as a source of life. On the north coast of Brittany, France, where the family lived, Conti's mother used the local fishermen's lives as educational material for the girl and her younger brother. Little Anita didn't go to school—the Caracotchians' money, background, cosmopolitanism, and spirit of independence enabled her to skip it. At the close of this idyllic childhood—spent from one cruise to another, one port of call to another, going from one learned uncle to another, rich, uncle—Anita might have found herself trapped by a paralyzing nostalgia for a lost paradise. As it happened, she managed to make the most of her years as a wealthy, youthful dropout.

Encouraged to learn a trade, she became a fine bookbinder and soon built up a fashionable clientele. She married a French diplomat, Marcel Conti, and then began writing for women's magazines. In short, she had a fairly conventional start in adult life—except that Madame Conti's articles did not discuss fashion or cooking, but described the wretched health standards of Brittany's commercial

Pages 220 and 221: Shrimp fishing at G'Bèsia, Guinea, in 1945; Anita Conti in Guinea, 1945–49.

Above, clockwise: A freighter off the coast of Newfoundland; Conti in the French navy during World War II, 1941; landing a shark in Guinea.

Facing page: Anita Conti on board a trawler, *Le Bois Rosé,* off Labrador, 1952; processing the fish on a trawler off Newfoundland.

oyster beds. Discussing such subjects, she found her voice: for this young woman, the call of the sea had a resolutely technical—one might even say "down to earth"—ring. Thus Conti landed a job with France's scientific bureau of fisheries (OSTPM, the forerunner of today's IFREMER, Institut Français de Recherche pour l'Exploitation de la Mer). Initially she was hired as a "propaganda officer"—that is to say, press attaché—but soon became a member of sea-going missions aboard the *Président Théodore Tissier,* France's first government-funded oceanographic research vessel. Impressed by Conti's self-taught expertise, the director of the OSTPM, Édouard Le Danois, asked her to take measurements and samples alongside her observation of fishing techniques. Thus they could steadily build up a data bank of information liable to supply answers to future problems in the fishing sector. Conti sailed northward, toward Newfoundland, Iceland, Spitsbergen, and beyond.

But she was recalled to France when World War II broke out. She offered to contribute her expertise on ocean currents to a minesweeping expedition that she knew was about to sail. It was composed of converted fishing boats (whose hulls were more difficult to detect by mines, because made of wood). The offer was rejected because women were not allowed to embark on military vessels. Once again, however, Madame Conti's unique skills were recognized, and a special decree allowed the rules to be bent for her. "We did this job in a state of total mania!" she wrote of her crew, which fished mines out of the sea the way trawlers fished sole. "We had to be completely crazy, crazy with fear and the fun of being able to say to ourselves, 'We'd better get this one or we'll blow ourselves sky-high!'"

Upon France's sudden defeat, it was not hard for Conti to flee her occupied country—she simply embarked on a trawler, *Le Volontaire,* heading for French colonies in Africa. From 1941 to 1943, still answering to the OSTPM but in fact working for the expatriate French government in Algiers, she sailed the African coasts on ships charged with supplying the allied armies and civilians with fish. She trained independent fishermen, suggested improvements in local techniques, defined methods of capture and conservation, set up fisheries, and installed smoking and curing installations. Faithful to her policy of being useful—thereby a worthy heir to the female explorers of the previous century—Conti promoted wider knowledge of the virtues of shark liver, which was particularly rich in vitamins.

In 1947, the new governor of Dakar put an end to her mission. Conti then attempted to start a commercial fishery, but quickly withdrew once she realized she could not reconcile her insatiable scientific curiosity with the business requirements of her partners. The sea called once again. As a perpetual hitchhiker, she spent the

rest of her life hopping from one trawler to another, sailing from Saint-Pierre to Dakar and from Venice to Conakry. When asked how she managed to get invited aboard so easily, she replied, "I understood right away that you should never bother sailors, so I simply made sure I was never hungry, never thirsty, never hot, never cold, never seasick, and never asked to wash—in short, I just took care of myself." By becoming an invisible little wraith, a ship's mascot, a sailors' madonna, she managed to sail all the world's oceans—camera in hand. Conti was not an art photographer, she simply cast an attentive, interested, and fond gaze on the fishermen that other people saw as brutish, but whom she could make smile for the lens. The view is so realistic that beholders of her photos can almost smell the wrack. Although conceived as a documentary record, her pictures are some of the most beautiful ever taken of the fishing industry.

In the late 1950s, it seemed as though she could finally set her sea chest on land and profit from the honors she had earned—for two years she worked alongside Captain Jacques-Yves Cousteau at the Musée Océanographique in Monaco, compiling a catalogue of poorly known marine species. "And then she simply vanished," said Cousteau, who probably couldn't get over the fact that a woman to whom he was offering recognition had decided to bow out. In fact, Conti had left to carry out aquaculture experiments in the Venetian lagoon. And then she set sail again—more trawlers, more sailors, more photos, and a few books.

It was not until the early 1980s, already past the age of eighty, that Conti finally came ashore, alone and modest. Fortunately, a

young illustrator who specialized in marine subjects, Laurent Giraud, looked her up and helped her—now aged eighty-seven—to file her archives: forty thousand photographs, some ten films, her ship's logs, her correspondence. Giraud also helped to set up a non-profit association (Cap sur Anita Conti¹), and the town to which she had retired, Douarnenez, agreed to showcase the newly discovered treasure. This new fame allegedly amused the retired oceanographer, who found it hard to understand why such old, obsolete photos should be sanctified. "Life moves on, even on the threshold of death," she used to say. "Living is always a surprise. Nothing lasts forever, everything changes, which is so delightful."

At her death in 1997, the finest tribute paid to her was uttered by a captain from Newfoundland, Jean Recher. "Anita was like an older sister to sailors. An older sister who had to raise a big family after the mother had died."

Facing page: Unloading a manta ray onto the dock at Conakry, Guinea, in 1945; net fishing in Dahomey, 1944–47.

Above: Anita Conti on board the oceanographic vessel, *Président Théodore Tissier*, in the Bay of Biscay, 1959.

Above and facing page: A storm in Newfoundland;
sailors on the trawler *Merr-Gwen*, off the coast
of Mauritania, 1942.

The horizon constantly retreats

Photos in the crew's quarters. Unlikely setting, lit on both sides by the pale eyes of two portholes. The bunks seem to be carved into the hull. In the middle is a table cluttered with an amazing jumble of coffee pots, cups, a phonograph, potato peelings, tobacco pouches, and crumpled clothes. On the benches are exhausted men, backs bent in weariness, who sit—or rather, collapse. . . . Men? No, not quite.

Beings deprived of their families, bodies packed in clothing that leaves only hands and faces visible. And when it's really cold outside, only the eyes of those faces show any life. So the men are no more than gestures and gazes, shut up in metallic jails driven by two hundred and fifty horsepower. These men, whether of inquiring intelligence or stubborn energy, whether refined or vulgar in thought, are always

just doppelgangers, in a way. Their souls are elsewhere. Above us, space. Below us, a mirror. And Viking works within its circle. Neither past nor future exists at sea—the trace of the wake vanishes. There's an eternal second, which is the center, while the horizon we chase constantly retreats, and nothing halts—ever.

Ship's log from the *Viking*, quoted in *Anita Conti, Dame de la mer* (Paris: Éditions Revue Noire, 2001).

City Girl Feels Safer
Alone in Gorilla Wilds

"*F*lushed with the glory and the triumph of my BSc., excited by the publicity which I received as the First Woman Graduate in Mining Engineering from the University of Wisconsin [this was 1926], and generally on top of the world, I completely forgot the reason for my acquiring that extraordinary diploma and actually took a job with a mining company."

Knowing How to Be Presumptuous

Yet the reason was perhaps as unusual as the degree itself. A few years earlier, in 1923, when she about to enroll in the English literature department, one of Emily Hahn's teachers proclaimed forthrightly in front of his class that a woman's brain was "incapable of grasping mechanics or higher mathematics." The teacher should not have been surprised that young Emily, called "Mickey" by her friends, would take the bait. At age eighteen, she was already planning to cross the American continent by car, along with a female friend who also came from a good family in Saint Louis, Missouri.

Hahn was nevertheless soon fed up with prospecting for oil, since her gender restricted her to an office job largely beneath her abilities. She abandoned this career to lead horseback tours in the Santa Fe area, then became a geology teacher in New York. There, in 1930, she found an opportunity to go to Africa: she was to accompany a cargo of medicine that the Red Cross was sending to its agent in the Congo, a certain Patrick Putman, the scion of an old Boston family who had created a scandal by marrying, during an academic voyage organized by Harvard, a woman from the Mangbetu tribe.

Hahn arrived in Putnam's territory to discover that he had not one, but three African wives—along with a somewhat eccentric, not to say tyrannical, personality. She nevertheless remained for two years in the bush hospital run by Putnam, stubborn and involved, until the day he went too far: when she asked him to help her trim her hair, Putnam told her she would either have to let it grow or shave it like African women. "No halfway measures any more! And that goes for you as well as the *other girls*. . . . clippers or nothing!"

Hahn left camp the next day. She had a plan, nurtured for some time, and now decided to put it into action: she would cross Africa

Pages 228 and 229: Comic strip from a New York newspaper, recounting Emily Hahn's adventures, August 14, 1933; and a portrait of Hahn.

Above: Postcard from the Congo.

Facing page: The port of Hong Kong in 1930; an opium den; a portrait of Hahn's lover, Chinese poet Sinmay Zau.

from west to east until she reached Lake Kivu. It meant traveling through eight hundred miles of tropical forest. The young American woman, wearing trousers and bush hat, took up this challenge in style.

Yet Africa still had things to be frightened of: crocodiles, herds of elephants, difficulties in finding food, the risk of desertion by porters, and even of slave hunters. Hahn, meanwhile, decided to travel light. Having left suddenly, she had neither supplies nor exact itinerary. And she brushed off various warnings. "All this I ignored," she said, "because in the Congo in those days, if you listened to local warnings you never got anything done. You had to possess a strong conceit. If you didn't believe down to your bones that you always knew best, and that Nature was sure to smile on *your* undertakings, whatever she might do to those of others, you would have to give up."

Up to that point, no female traveler would ever have admitted to such lack of preparation, for fear of it being viewed as a failing of her sex. Once again, however, times were changing. Endowed with solid physical stamina, with a confidence in the future that stemmed from her upbringing, and a sunny smile, Hahn put herself body and soul into the hands of her African guides, who were in fact chosen more carefully than her declarations of unconcern might suggest. "There were no roads yet through the trees; there was just a system of pathways that were—at least half of them—elephant tracks. Apart from my head boy, Shabani, I needed a guide to figure them out. Mine was a Pygmy, whose people, of course, knew all the ways of elephants. You could always rely on a Pygmy."

Chinese smoking Opium.

Far from being a terminus, her arrival at Lake Kivu was a point of departure. More than ever convinced of her ability, Hahn became a wanderer—indeed, a figure of scandal, as fate would have it. In this she fit the mythical image of the American adventuress of the interwar period, such as movies and novels presented her: free in everything, a blend of elegance and provocation, ready for any experience. In 1935, Hahn traveled with her sister to Japan, then visited China; there she settled in Shanghai, where she became the concubine of a Chinese poet, Sinmay Zau. She also became hooked on opium, and got to know Mao Zedong and the Song sisters. Then she moved on to Hong Kong, where she fell in love with a married man, Charles Boxer, head of British military intelligence—another shocking affair. It hardly mattered: one week before Pearl Harbor, Hahn gave birth to a daughter, Carola. Then the Japanese arrived,

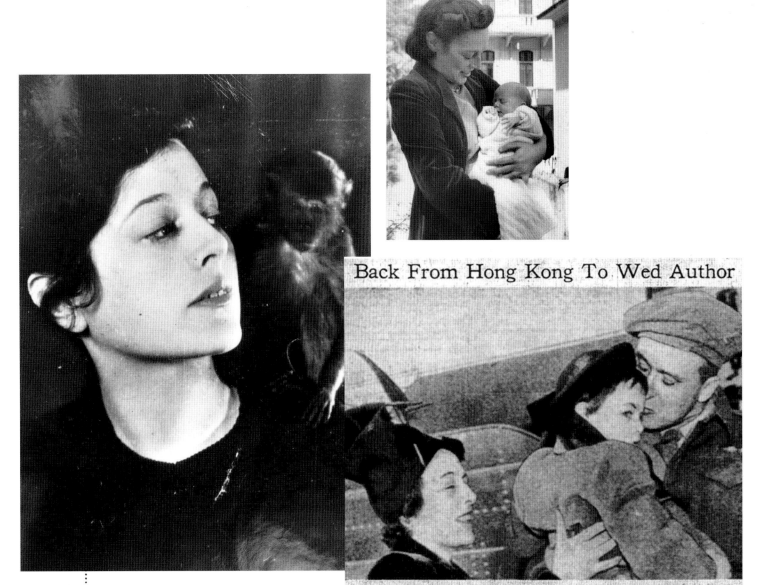

Back From Hong Kong To Wed Author

MAJOR CHARLES BOXER, AUTHOR EMILY HAHN AND THEIR CHILD
Excited cries of "Daddy, Daddy," greeted him.

Above: Hahn and her pet monkey, 1929; with her daughter Carola in Hong Kong, October 1941; Hahn and Carola greeting Charles Boxer at the airport in New York, November 22, 1945.

Facing page: Emily "chatting" with monkeys in 1978 as part of her research into animal communication.

Boxer was arrested, and all the British were interned or placed under surveillance. Despite the risks to her baby and herself, Hahn joined a smuggling ring designed to circumvent the strict rationing imposed by the occupying army. Then, thanks to her knowledge of Asian culture, she managed to become friendly with Japanese officers, the better to help her friends—which would later earn her the suspicion of being an enemy agent when she finally returned to the United States.

After the war, Hahn behaved more conventionally. She married her British lover, and she devoted her energy to her writing career—her own life provided such a wealth of material that she could live from it comfortably for a long time. As she grew older, she specialized in writing about animals, with a notable interest in promoting the study of animal communication. It was a subject she knew well, in her own way, since for many years she used to go around with a monkey on her shoulder. The most famous of her monkeys, called Mr. Mills, used to wear a mink coat—just for the fun of *creating a scandal.*

Wistfulness and vitriol

British historian Harriet Sargeant wrote that when she began researching the 1930s for her book on Shanghai, she discovered that "nearly everyone I interviewed had an anecdote about Emily Hahn. Men recalled her wistfully; women with vitriol." Although Shanghai's foreign community, about 60,000 people in the mid-1930s, had no shortage of larger-than-life characters, Mickey Hahn had emerged as one of the best known and most visible. In fact, when film director Josef von Sternberg . . . visited Shanghai, he sent Mickey a huge bouquet of flowers and took her and Sinmay to lunch. Such was the extent and nature of Mickey's celebrity.

Ken Cuthbertson, *Nobody Said Not to Go* (Boston: Faber & Faber, 1998).

233

Indefatigable!

Most unexpectedly, adventure doesn't kill female explorers—it prolongs their lives.

Most of them lived to be old, indeed very old. Ella Maillart, Alexandra David-Néel, Freya Stark, Odette du Puigaudeau, Anita Conti, Emily Hahn, and many others lived into their nineties. A few even made it to one hundred, and died peacefully in their beds, surrounded by loved ones, at home.

At home?

Right from the start, trailblazing women's relationship to "home" was as ambivalent as it was complicated. While some of them waited until the Lord freed them from familial duty before leaving hearth and home, others couldn't bear to be without their relatives, and thus took their hearth with them, dragging their relations in their wake (with a slight preference for mothers and close female relatives such as aunts, nieces, or sisters).

Isabella Bird pioneered this path, admitting that she could never have traveled the globe nor even survived if she had been cut off from her roots, amputated from her other half—namely, her sister Henrietta. Isabella's adventure, and the survival of her work, rested on a monologue addressed to Henrietta, the soul mate who remained at home, expressed in all the letters Isabella sent from the four corners of the earth, recording her enthusiasms and confessing her anxieties. Miss Traveler Bird needed to confide endlessly in Miss Stay-at-Home Bird, creating a symbiosis between two parts of a single whole, a marriage of Adventure and Home.

Alexine Tinne, who couldn't imagine plunging deep into African deserts without her mother, felt the same need for unity, the same desire for osmosis between her emotional worlds. Her perfect harmony with her mother and aunt, the two female mentors of her childhood, assumed full scope when sharing the discoveries and emotions of traveling. Fanny Stevenson, meanwhile, didn't coax her mother to the South Pacific, she went one better: she enticed her *mother-in-law* to live among the natives of the Samoan Islands. As a symbol of the link between past and present, Fanny chose a widow who had never known anything but the cold existence of middle-class Edinburgh. Margaret Stevenson, "Aunt Maggie," was a respectable old lady when she arrived in Samoa but she loved the experience. It might be added that Fanny, familiar with this type of sport, had already braved the South Seas with her own children, notably dragging her daughter, Belle, into the unknown. Finally, Isabelle Eberhardt, a fresh convert to Islam, led her mother, Nathalie de Moerder, down the road to the Koran and the discovery of Muhammad; today de Moerder lies in an Islamic cemetery beneath a tombstone with her Muslim name, Fatima Manubia.

This determination not to leave cradle and loved ones behind could be a very costly decision. Fanny Stevenson lost one of her two sons during a voyage. Alexine Tinne's mother, aunt, and two chambermaids died of fever in wretched conditions. Neither Stevenson nor Tinne ever got over their feelings of guilt. Such feelings prevented the former from ever returning to Indiana, the latter to Holland. But they were among the few travelers who refused to go home.

How many chose, as their final home, a land worlds away from their roots? Not many. Women adventurers don't generally choose to live in foreign lands, nor does death catch them in the field. True, Isabelle Eberhardt would die far, far away from her native Switzerland. As would Tinne, Mary Kingsley, and Gertrude Bell. These four grand ladies' lives were halted in mid-stride by human violence or natural catastrophe. But what about the others? The others—all the others—returned home. Even David-Néel, even Maillart, and even Anita Conti!

And then?

After enjoying such rich experiences and vast horizons, toward what goals could they devote their terrific energy? How could they survive once they returned to the world of their childhood, a world simultaneously so familiar and so foreign? Were they overwhelmed by nostalgia? Or tempted to put an end to it all? What did they do with themselves?

All these questions have a single answer: they carried on.

All carried on the voyage, pursued the absolute quest that had marked them forever, and accomplished—via writing—the crucial task for which they had decided to return home: *to pass on what they had learned.*

This need to pass the torch explains why several of them, seeking to establish traditional family ties late in life, would adopt a chosen son or daughter, making him or her their legal heir. That is why Conti and David-Néel selected spiritual heirs from among the young people who wanted to support their work and promote their oeuvre. "On the whole," admitted Freya Stark, "age comes more gently to those who have some doorway into . . . learning-regions where the years are scarcely noticed and the young and old can meet in a pale, truthful light."

Lectures, publications, exhibitions: by sharing their acquired knowledge with young people, these trailblazers were retracing their own steps, organizing their ideas, and structuring their memories. They were thereby celebrating, once again, the triumph of the god of intelligence and open-mindedness. This was an adventure that they could live and re-live from home.

They no longer needed an "Elsewhere" in order to go ever higher, ever further; their quest beyond all known worlds; to reach the goal of all voyages, in serenity. Blessed were those who achieved their dreams. Blessed were those who died, while having lived.

Graced by these two magnificent blessings, did these great women explorers ever think of the numerous women whose wishes were never granted? The silent women, the invisible women, the forgotten women? All those pioneers that history and the world have decided to forget. The time has come to pay tribute to such women.

Who were they, these travelers whose adventures may have surpassed in scope the audacity of famous heroines such as Gertrude Bell and Alexandra David-Néel? They were the starving Irishwomen of the 1850s, the Sicilian women driven from their infertile lands in the 1890s, the orphan girls deported to Australia in the early twentieth century, the wives of modest civil servants dispatched to the ends of the colonial empire. All of them were caught up in the vast maelstrom of peoples that marked the century of emigration and colonization from 1850 to 1950.

Some of these obscure pioneers pushed their husbands to seek a better future elsewhere, others left on their own to find a job or a husband. They walked for weeks, even months, they slept in the lower decks of unhealthy steamers, they lived in tents, on the beach, in wagons. They defended, alone, their children on a little ranch in the badlands, rifle in hand. They waited for weeks on end in a solitary hut in a remote forest for an army husband to return from an inspection tour. They ran plantations in New Guinea, they crossed the Pacific to meet a mail-order husband seven thousand miles from home, they set up dry-goods stores for Klondike miners, they became nurses in the Kalahari.

We know none, or almost none, of these adventurers' names. We can cite no books, because they didn't write—except, perhaps, to their families. And since they didn't write, people think they never existed—at least as individuals. For historians, they were just part of a vague, unidentified mass of global emigration. For everyone else, they were swallowed up by the void, fell through a hole in the collective awareness. Otherwise how can we explain the fact that, in upper-class society in Paris and London, the image of women was one of utmost fragility—a true lady fainted at the least emotion, was unable to go outdoors at the least indisposition, and was sick with shame at the least sight of male flesh—at the very moment that that deserts, oceans, and jungles were witnessing the arrival of contingents of barefoot women, complexions darkened by the sun, muscles hardened by walking, riding, and carrying a rifle?

What a shame that, among these legions of nameless foot soldiers, so few were able to keep a log of their daily exploits. The twists and turns of their modest tales were probably a match for the accounts of the most famous male explorers. And probably once they, too, attained a ripe old age, surrounded by countless grandchildren—for they were as fertile as they were hardy—they would have agreed with Anita Conti, who at eighty-one exclaimed:

"Women are indefatigable!"

A. L. & C. M.

Notes

Catalina de Erauso
1. The most recent adaptation is a novel by Eduardo Manet, *La Conquistadora* (Paris: Robert Laffont, 2006).

Aphra Behn
1. Janet Todd, *The Secret Life of Aphra Behn* (London: Pandora Press, 2000).
2. *Oroonoko* (Oxford: Oxford World Classics, 1994).

Isabel Godin des Odonais
1. The first account was by Jean Godin des Odonais himself. Charles de La Condamine had asked him to write a report on his wife's adventure. It was this text that served as the source for all successive chroniclers such as Marie Dronsart, *Les Grandes Voyageuses* (Paris: Hachette, 1894) and Félix de Grandmaison, *Un Drame inconnu: aventures de Madame Godin des Odonais, née Isabelle de Grandmaison y Bruno* (Saint-Amand-Montrond, 1830). Marc Blancpain, author of *Le Plus Long Amour* (Paris: Éditions Tallandier, 1971), also relied on the information supplied by Jean Godin.
2. Jean Godin des Odonais, *Relation du Voyage de Madame Godin, son Épouse*, letter to Charles de La Condamine, 1778.

The Blessings of a Good Thick Skirt
1. A surveying instrument used to measure an angle in relation to the horizon, in order to establish position (that is, a land-based equivalent of a sextant).

Ida Pfeiffer
1. Queen Ranavalona, who had reigned since 1827, was very hostile to Europeans. The French found her youngest son to be a more amenable interlocutor, and they therefore sought to overthrow the queen and install her son on the throne. Pfeiffer, who was traveling with some French people, incautiously sided against Ranavalona.

Florence Baker
1. Pat Shipman, *To the Heart of the Nile* (London: Transworld Publishers, 2005). A version that sticks closer to family legend is offered by a Baker descendent, Anne Baker, in *Morning Star* (London: William Kimber, 1972).
2. The travelers were Charles Delme-Radcliffe and the anthropologist F. K. Girling.

Isabella Bird
1. Pat Barr, *A Curious Life for a Lady: The Story of Isabella Bird* (New York: Doubleday, 1970).

May French-Sheldon
1. May French-Sheldon, *Sultan to Sultan* (1892) (Manchester: Manchester University Press, 1999).

Jane Dieulafoy
1. The Dieulafoy articles that originally appeared in *Le Tour du Monde* have been anthologized and published as *En mission chez les immortels* (Paris: Éditions Phébus, 1990).

Fanny Stevenson
1. Quoted by Alexandra Lapierre, *Fanny Stevenson, Entre passion et liberté* (Paris: Robert Laffont, 1993).

Mary Kingsley
1. Lecture given to the Cheltenham Ladies College, quoted by Mary Davies on the Internet site of the Royal African Society (http://www.royalafricansociety.org).

Fanny Bullock Workman
1. French for "never mind!"

Margaret Fountaine
1. Margaret Fountaine's diaries have been published under the title, *Love Among the Butterflies: The Travels and Adventures of a Victorian Lady*, with an introduction by W. F. Cater (London: William Collins & Sons, 1980).

Daisy Bates
1. This research was published by Julia Blackburn as *Daisy Bates in the Desert* (London: Vintage Books, 1995).

Isabelle Eberhardt
1. In 1872, Paschkoff traveled from Russia to Palmyra with a caravan of thirty-three mules and thirty-five camels. See Lydie Paschkoff, "Voyage en Asie Mineure dans l'ancienne capitale de Mithridate," in *Le Tour du Monde*, vol. 1, 1889.
2. Isabelle Eberhardt, "Impressions du Sud-oranais," in *Isabelle Eberhardt, Lettres et journaliers* (Paris: Actes Sud, 1987).

Charmian Kittredge
1. Quoted in Russ Kingman, *A Pictorial Life of Jack London* (New York: Crown Publishers, 1979).

Alexandra David-Néel
1. Jean Chalon, *Le lumineux destin d'Alexandra David-Néel* (Paris: Perrin, 1998).

Evelyn Cheesman
1. Evelyn Cheesman, *Time Well Spent* (London: The Travel Book Club, 1960).

Rosita Forbes
1. The book by Rosita Forbes, *The Secret of the Sahara Kufara*, was republished by Long Rider's Guild Press, London, in 2000.

Margaret Mead
1. Edward Sapir.
2. See Lois W. Banner, *Intertwined Lives: Margaret Mead and Ruth Benedict and their Circle* (New York: Knopf, 2003).
3. Margaret Mead, *Blackberry Winter* (London: Argus & Robertson, 1973).

Ella Maillart
1. The figures Maillart saw were the giant Buddhas at Bamiyan, demolished by the Taliban fifty years later.

Odette du Puigaudeau
1. Monique Vérité, *Odette du Puigaudeau, une Bretonne au désert* (Paris: Éditions Jean Picollec, 1992).
2. Ibid.

Anita Conti
1. Cap sur Anita Conti, 30 rue du Commandant-Fernand, 29100 Douarnenez, France.

Selected Bibliography

Al Ahram (Egyptian daily).

Anita Conti, dame de la mer. Paris: Éditions Revue Noire, 2001. Exhibition catalog.

Association Cap sur Anita Conti. *Anita Conti, Femme océan.* Video cassette.

Baker, Anne. *Morning Star.* London: William Kimber, 1972.

Baker, Samuel. *The Albert N'Yanza: Great Basin of the Nile and Explorations of the Nile Sources.* London: Echo Library, 2005.

Barr, Pat. *A Curious Life for a Lady: The Story of Isabella Bird.* New York: Doubleday, 1970.

Birkett, Dea. *Off the Beaten Tracks.* London: National Portrait Gallery, 2004. Exhibition catalog.

Blackburn, Julia. *Daisy Bates in the Desert.* London: Vintage Books, 1995.

Blixen, Karen [Isak Dinesen]. *Out of Africa.* New York: Random House, 1952.

Bly, Nellie. *Around the World in Seventy-Two Days.* New York: The Pictorial Weekly Company, 1890, republished, New Delhi: Indialog Publications, 2003.

Frank Boas to Margaret Mead, July 14, 1925. Letters of Margaret Mead. Library of Congress, Washington, DC.

David-Néel, Alexandra. *Journal de voyage.* Vol. 1. Paris: Plon, 1975.

David-Néel, Alexandra. *Journal de voyage.* Vol. 2. Paris: Plon, 1976.

Chalon, Jean. *Le lumineux destin d'Alexandra David-Néel.* Paris: Perrin, 1998.

Cheesman, Evelyn. *Time Well Spent.* London: The Travel Book Club, 1960.

Cuthbertson, Ken. *Nobody Said Not to Go: The Life, Loves and Adventures of Emily Hahn.* Boston: Faber & Faber, 1998.

Dieulafoy, Jane. *En mission chez les immortels, Journal des fouilles de Suse, 1884-1886.* Paris: Éditions Phébus, 1990.

Errera, Eglal. *Isabelle Eberhardt, Lettres et journaliers.* Paris: Actes Sud, 1987.

Dronsart, Marie. *Les Grandes Voyageuses.* Paris: Hachette, 1894.

Du Puigaudeau, Odette. *Pieds nus à travers la Mauritanie.* Paris: Phébus, 2003.

Forbes, Rosita. *The Secret of the Sahara Kufara.* London: Long Rider's Guild Press, 2000.

Fountaine, Margaret. Introduction by W. F. Cater. *Love Among the Butterflies: The Travels and Adventures of a Victorian Lady.* London: William Collins & Sons, 1980.

Frank, Katherine. *A Voyager Out: The Life of Mary Kingsley.* London: Hamish Hamilton, 1987.

French-Sheldon, May. *Sultan to Sultan* (1892). Manchester: Manchester University Press, 1999.

Geniesse, Jane F. *Passionate Nomad: The Life of Freya Stark.* London: Modern Library, 2001.

Gladstone, Penelope. *Travels of Alexine.* London: John Murray, 1970.

Godin des Odonais, Jean. *Relation du Voyage de Madame Godin, son Épouse* (letter to Charles de La Condamine). Paris, 1778.

Goodman, Susan. *Gertrude Bell.* London: Berg, 1985.

Gran-Aymeric, Ève and Jean Gran-Aymeric. *Jane Dieulafoy, Une vie d'homme.* Paris: Perrin, 1991.

Johnson, Osa. *I Married Adventure: The Life and Adventures of Martin and Osa Johnson.* New York: Willima Morrow, 1940.

Kingman, Russ. *A Pictorial Life of Jack London.* New York: Crown Publishers, 1979.

Kingsley, Mary. Lecture given to the Cheltenham Ladies College. *See quotation by Mary Davies on the Internet site of the Royal African Society,* http://www.royalafricansociety.org

Kingsley, Mary. *Travels in West Africa.* Mineola, NY: Dover, 2003; reprint of 1897 edition.

Lapierre, Alexandra. *Fanny Stevenson, Entre passion et liberté.* Paris: Robert Laffont, 1993.

Maillart, Ella. *The Cruel Way.* London: Virago Press, 1986.

Maillart, Ella. *Ti-Puss.* Paris: Payot, 2002.

Maillart, Ella. *Forbidden Journey from Peking to Kashmir.* London: Marlboro Press, 2003.

Maillart, Ella. See http://www.ellamaillart.ch

Malraux, André. *Oeuvres complètes. Vol 2.* Paris: Gallimard, 1996. Quoted by Sylvain Venayre, *La gloire et l'aventure, genèse d'une mystique moderne, 1850-1940.* Paris: Aubier, 2002.

Mead, Margaret. *Coming of Age in Samoa.* Harmondsworth: Pelican Books, 1928.

Mehew, Ernest, ed. *Selected Letters of Robert Louis Stevenson.* New Haven: Yale University Press, 2001.

Middleton, Dorothy. *Victorian Lady Travellers.* London: Routledge, 1965.

Miermont, Dominique-Laure. *Annemarie Schwarzenbach ou le mal d'Europe.* Paris: Payot, 2004.

Moorehead, Caroline. *Freya Stark.* Harmondsworth: Penguin, 1986.

Pfeiffer, Ida. *A Lady's Voyage Round the World.* Translated from the German by Mrs. Percy Sinnett (1851). London: Century, 1988.

Polk, Milbry and Mary Tiegreen. *Women of Discovery.* New York: Clarkson Potter, 2001.

Reverzy, Catherine. *Femmes d'aventure: du rêve à la réalisation de soi.* Paris: Odile Jacob, 2001.

Sackville-West, Vita. *Twelve Days: An Account of a Journey Across the Bakhtiari Mountains.* New York: Doubleday, 1928.

Sanchez, Nellie. *The Life of Mrs. Robert Louis Stevenson.* New York: Charles Scribner's Sons, 1920.

Seacole, Mary. *The Wonderful Adventures of Mary Seacole in Many Lands.* New York: Oxford University Press, 1990.

Shipman, Pat. *To the Heart of the Nile.* London: Transworld Publishers Ltd., 2005.

Stone, Irving. *Jack London, Sailor on Horseback.* New York: Doubleday, 1938.

Thurman, Judith. *Isak Dinesen: The Life of Karen Blixen.* Harmondsworth: Penguin, 1986.

Todd, Janet. *The Secret Life of Aphra Behn.* London: Pandora Press, 2000.

Vérité, Monique. *Odette du Puigaudeau, une Bretonne au désert.* Paris: Éditions Jean Picollec, 1992.

Weber, Olivier. *Je suis de nulle part: Sur les traces d'Ella Maillart.* Paris: Payot, 2004.

Winstone, Harry V. F. *Gertrude Bell.* London: Jonathan Cape, 1978.

Photographic Credits

Cover: Martin and Osa Johnson Safari Museum / **title page:** Anita Conti, agence Vu / **Contents:** Bibliothèque nationale de France / **page 5:** private collection / **page 6:** The British Museum, London / **page 9:** musée d'Orsay, Paris, photo RMN, Hervé Lewandowski / **page 10:** Bibliothèque nationale de France, Paris, Lauros, Giraudon, Bridgeman Giraudon / **page 11:** Marie Dronsart, *Les Grandes Voyageuses*, Hachette & Cie, 1898 / **page 12:** Mercedes Monastery, Cuzco, Peru, Paul Maeyaert, Bridgeman Giraudon / **page 13:** Map of Cuzco: Marie Dronsart, *Les Grandes Voyageuses*, Hachette & Cie, 1898. Cordillère landscape: private collection, Bridgeman Giraudon / **page 14:** Bibliothèque nationale de France, Paris, archives Charmet, Bridgeman Giraudon / **page 15:** St. Hilda's College, Oxford, Bridgeman Giraudon / **page 16:** Hanged slave: private collection, Stapleton collection, Bridgeman Giraudon. Surinam plantation: Bibliothèque des Arts décoratifs, Paris, archives Charmet, Bridgeman Giraudon. Slave family: Stapleton collection, Bridgeman Giraudon / **page 17:** National Portrait Gallery, London / **page 18:** Bibliothèque Sainte-Geneviève, Paris, archives Charmet, Bridgeman Giraudon / **page 19:** Bibliothèque nationale de France / **page 20:** View of Lima: Stapleton collection, Bridgeman Giraudon. Brazilian forest: private collection, Whitford & Hughes, London, Bridgeman Giraudon. Tapir hunt: private collection, Bridgeman Giraudon / **page 21:** Marie Dronsart, *Les Grandes Voyageuses*, Hachette & Cie, 1898 / **page 22:** Royal Botanical Gardens, Kew / **page 23:** Pat Barr, *A Curious Life for a Lady*, Secker & Warburg, 1970 / **pages 28–29:** Time-Life Pictures, Getty Images / **page 30:** *Le Tour du monde, nouveau journal des voyages*, Librairie Hachette et Cie, Paris, 1861 / **page 31:** Marie Dronsart, *Les Grandes Voyageuses*, Hachette & Cie, 1898 / **pages 32–33:** Ida Pfeiffer, *Voyage d'une femme autour du monde*, Mégard et Cie, 1888 / **page 34:** Marie Dronsart, *Les Grandes Voyageuses*, 1898 / **page 35:** Ida Pfeiffer, *Visit to Iceland*, Ingram, Cook and Co., 1852 / **page 36:** *Le Tour du monde, nouveau journal des voyages*, Librairie Hachette et Cie, Paris, 1871 / **page 37:** Imagno, Getty Images / **page 38:** Postcard: private collection. Engraving: Marie Dronsart, *Grandes Voyageuses*, Hachette, 1898 / **page 39:** private collection / **page 40:** Portrait of Alexine Tinne: Marie Dronsart, *Les Grandes Voyageuses*, Hachette, 1898. Marshlands of Bahr el-Ghazal: *Le Tour du monde, nouveau journal des voyages*, Librairie Hachette et Cie, Paris,1871 / **page 41:** *Le Tour du monde, nouveau journal des voyages*, Librairie Hachette et Cie, Paris, 1871 / **page 42:** Wilfried Westphal, *Tochter des Sultans*, Torbecke, Stuttgard, all rights reserved / **page 43:** private collection / **page 44:** private collection, Bridgeman Giraudon / **page 45:** collection Amoret Tanner, Fotolibra / **page 46:** Engraving of Kingston: private collection, photo: Christie's Images, Bridgeman Giraudon. Portrait of Mary Seacole: private collection, Bridgeman Giraudon / **page 47:** Panama: the New-York Historical Society collection, Bridgeman Giraudon. Forest in Panama: all rights reserved by agence Roger-Viollet / **pages 48–49:** private collection, Bridgeman Giraudon / **page 50:** Soldiers' portraits: photo RMN, all rights reserved. Port of Bakalva: Roger Fenton, Getty Images / **page 51:** Museum of London / **page 52:** Bibliothèque nationale de France / **page 53:** Bibliothèque nationale de France / **page 54:** all rights reserved by agence Roger-Viollet / **page 55:** Sir Samuel W. Baker, *Le Lac Albert*, Hachette, 1869 / **page 56:** Royal Geographical Society / **page 57:** Sir Samuel W. Baker, *Le Lac Albert*, Hachette, 1869 / **page 58:** Isabella Bird, *A Lady's Life in the Rocky Mountains*, Virago Travellers, 1982 / **page 59:** Royal Geographical Society / **page 60:** Bibliothèque nationale de France / **page 61:** Bibliothèque nationale de France: Mary Dronsart, *Les Grandes Voyageuses*, Hachette & Cie, 1898 / **page 62:** Isabella Bird on horseback: Pat Barr, *A Curious Life for a Lady*, Secker & Warburg, 1970. Colorado fur-traders: John K. Hillers, Corbis / **page 63:** private collection, Bridgeman Giraudon / **page 64:** Frances Elizabeth Williard, *Occupations for Women*, Cooper Union, New York, 1897 / **page 65:** Corbis / **page 66:** May French Sheldon, *Sultan to Sultan*, Arena Publishing, Boston, 1892, all rights reserved / **page 67:** private collection / **page 68:** May French Sheldon, *Sultan to Sultan*, Arena Publishing, Boston, 1892, all rights reserved / **page 69:** private collection / **page 70:** Royal Botanical Gardens, Kew / **pages 71–72:** Royal Botanical Gardens, Kew, Bridgeman Giraudon / **page 73:** private collection / **page 74:** *Le Tour du monde*, nouveau journal des voyages, Librairie Hachette et Cie, Paris, 1887 / **page 75:** photothèque Hachette Livre / **pages 76–77:** *Le Tour du monde, nouveau journal des voyages*, Librairie Hachette et Cie, Paris, 1883, 1888 / **page 78:** all rights reserved by agence Roger-Viollet / **page 79:** *Le Tour du monde, nouveau journal des voyages*, Librairie Hachette et Cie, Paris, 1886 / **page 80:** *Le Tour du monde, nouveau journal des voyages*, Librairie Hachette et Cie, Paris, 1887 / **page 81:** *Le Tour du monde, nouveau journal des voyages*, Librairie Hachette et Cie Paris, 1888 / **page 82:** private collection, Bridgeman Giraudon / **page 83:** Beinecke Rare Book and Manuscript Library, Yale University, all rights reserved / **page 84:** Robert Louis Stevenson on his boat: Hachette photos presse. Portrait of Fanny Stevenson: The Writers' Museum, Lady Stair's House, Edinburgh / **page 85:** all rights reserved by agence Roger-Viollet / **page 86:** The Writers' Museum, Lady Stair's House, Edinburgh / **page 87:** Rischgitz, Stringer, Getty Images / **pages 88–90:** Bibliothèque nationale de France, all rights reserved / **pages 91–92:** Reinhold Thiele, Stringer, Getty Images / **page 93:** Royal Geographical Society / **page 94:** Bibliothèque nationale de France / **page 95:** Topical Press Agency, Getty Images / **page 96:** Fanny on her bicycle in front of Indian monument: William Hunter Workman and Fanny Bullock, *Through Town and Jungle*, T. Fisher Unwin, London, 1904. Fanny in her tent: Bibliothèque nationale de France / **pages 97–99:** Bibliothèque nationale de France / **page 100:** reproduced by kind permission of the Huntington Library, San Marino, California /

Translated from the French by Deke Dusinberre
Design: Caroline Renouf
Typesetting: Claude-Olivier Four
Copyediting: Pippa Hurd
Proofreading: Chrisoula Petridis
Color Separation: Reproscan, Italy

Distributed in North America by Rizzoli International Publications, Inc.

Simultaneously published in French as *Elles ont conquis le monde*
© Flammarion, Paris, 2007

English-language edition
© Flammarion, 2007

87, quai Panhard et Levassor
75647 Paris Cedex 13

www.editions.flammarion.com

08 09 3 2

ISBN-13: 978-2-0803-0018-8

Dépôt légal: 09/2007

Printed in Singapore by Tien Wah Press